The Gray Witch's Grimoire

The Gray
Witch's
Grimoire

Amythyst Raine

MOON
BOOKS

Winchester, UK
Washington, USA

First published by Moon Books, 2012
Moon Books is an imprint of John Hunt Publishing Ltd., Laurel House, Station Approach,
Alresford, Hants, SO24 9JH, UK
office1@jhpbooks.net
www.johnhuntpublishing.com
www.moon-books.net

For distributor details and how to order please visit the 'Ordering' section on our website.

Text copyright: Amythyst Raine 2011

ISBN: 978 1 78099 273 0

A CIP catalogue record for this book is available from the British Library.

Design: Stuart Davies

Printed and bound by CPI Group (UK) Ltd, Croydon, CR0 4YY

We operate a distinctive and ethical publishing philosophy in all
areas of our business, from our global network of authors to
production and worldwide distribution.

CONTENTS

Book Blessing:
Upon these pages,
O Mother Goddess,
Bless the words You see.
Give them strength and power
To set my magic free.

The Gray Witch

'Are you a good witch or a bad witch?' So the popular line goes. And what would my answer be? I'm both and I'm neither. I'm caught somewhere in the middle, between the fluffy bunny and the wicked witch. I reside in that illusive uncategorized world of the gray witch.

The world of the gray witch has been largely avoided, misrepresented, or glossed over in various books geared gingerly towards 'protection magic'. These books, informative and well-written as they may be, have totally missed the spirit of the gray witch – who she really is, how she relates to the world of shadow and light, and exactly what she's willing to do to stand her ground.

In our society 'dark' is automatically viewed as 'evil'; and 'light' is automatically viewed as 'good'. We're expected to live completely within one realm and to totally avoid the other. This creates imbalance and is a great injustice to the true spirit of the ancient wise woman.

This book puts matters right and gives the public a view of just what the gray witch is – and what she isn't. The gray witch does not live in a world of chaos or unbridled black magic. She has a code of honor, a sense of propriety, and a relevance in today's society.

The gray witch abhors violence, hatred, and conflict as much as the next person; but she's not afraid to face these issues using the power she possesses to right a situation and reinstate balance. The gray witch doesn't flinch at the earthier aspects of her craft that send the fluffy bunnies running for cover, clinging to their illusion of a perfect white world. The gray witch, when faced with a dilemma that requires immediate action, doesn't waste time in nail-biting indecision; she sucks it up, acts decisively and swiftly, doing what she has to do, getting done what needs to be done – righting a wrong; breaking a curse – or casting one if it's needed; creating balance where there is imbalance, and justice where it's called for. She protects her family and loved ones with witchcraft, not apologizing for who or what she is, but reveling in the power that becomes her.

The gray witch follows the beat of her own drum; she's fiercely independent, the true essence of the wild-woman, untamable, awe-inspiring, and an awesome sight to behold. The gray witch is *not* a creature to be toyed with. But there's also another side to this witch, one that's often overlooked in the great debate of black and white – the gray witch is kind, loyal, loving, and gentle. She is blessed with a connection to nature and the Old Ways that comes from a much deeper place than the modern witchcraft of today.

This is the Gray Witch.

Embrace her individuality, applaud her courage, uphold her rights, and allow her to run free with the wild things…for this is where she belongs.

Blessed Be,

Lady Amythyst Raine

To Keep Silent

To Know
To Dare
To Will
To Keep Silent

Now is the time for you to learn the value of silence, the value of keeping the witches' secrets. Of the four rungs listed on the Witches' Ladder above, the last is the most important. At one time in history, maintaining silence meant the difference between life and death, between freedom and incarceration.

Witchcraft was illegal in Great Britain until 1950. This may seem like a relatively long time ago to some, but it's not. The last threatened use of the Witchcraft Act in England (against a medium) was in 1950. In 1951 the Witchcraft Act was repealed and replaced with the Fraudulent Mediums Act 1951. There are witches walking the world today, openly practicing their craft, who were born in this year – the year of enlightenment, it could be called.

It should be noted that witchcraft was illegal in the United States until 1985; and women are still being murdered in Africa and executed in the Middle East in these modern times for the practice of witchcraft. The slaughter of women in Africa for witchcraft, in fact, has become so widespread that secret safe houses have been established for their protection, and it is feared the female balance of the population will eventually be affected if these witch hunts do not stop.[1]

Although a witch will not be arrested in the United States today for practicing her craft, nor put to death for what and who she is, there is still a reason for secrecy, a reason for this rung upon the Witches' Ladder.

First, manifestation of magic, of your spell crafting, requires that the energies you have raised and the magic that you have cast be carefully guarded, lest it all dissipate into thin air. It must be your secret. And within this shroud of secrecy the magic will build and grow, increase in power and force, until it manifests within the real world – our world, the world of taste and touch, sight and smell.

But as powerful as this energy is, it's still fragile; and the one thing that can destroy it, scatter it, dissipate it, is revealing it. If you talk about the magic you are casting, it will not work. Every time you open your mouth and expose it to an individual, and then another, and another, the energy begins to fade, to grow weaker and weaker, thinner and thinner, until it evaporates into the ether, going back to its original state, to the place of its origin.

Guard your magic, the spells you cast, with silence.

Another reason for this rung upon the Witches' Ladder is to protect the magical workings and power of a coven. A coven member must value the importance of silence even more than a solitary witch, for the secrets that she keeps are not her own.

There may be coven members who practice witchcraft in secrecy, keeping their practice even from their closest family members. And then there are the spells cast by your coven; I told you what happens to magical energy when you speak of it, when you spread it thinner by sharing it. Honor the last rung on the Witches' Ladder, 'To Keep Silent', so you don't wind up being the weak link within your group, so you do not sabotage the magical workings of your coven.

Part 1

Knowledge

Magical Principles for the Gray Witch

1. Magic is natural, and the energies used to create magic come from natural sources: the earth, the planets, deities, spirits, stones, herbs, elements, and the will of the witch.

2. Try to bring harm to no one in the practice of your magic, but do not hesitate to use this magic for protection against enemies, energies, or circumstances that threaten you, your family members, and those you love.

3. The amount of time, energy, and effort you put into the practice of magic will show in the results.

4. Since magic is natural, the way in which it manifests will also be natural. Forget everything you've ever seen in movies or on TV. Real magic does not manifest with special effects.

    The successful results of spell casting may show their face with an incredible display of synchronicity; with a natural adjustment of choice, or thought, or action; with an unexpected opportunity that seems to come out of the blue; with a whisper in your ear; or with a quiet change of circumstance.

    This is how real magic works.

5. Most people believe you should never accept payment for casting spells. At first glance this looks like a good principle in general. But then, when you think about it from a different perspective, it takes on a different color.

    The magical practitioner deserves to be reimbursed for all the materials she uses to cast a spell and for the time she spends writing and preparing the spell itself. This is no different than paying a Protestant minister or a Catholic priest for their time and services. They don't work for free; why would you expect a magical practitioner, or a member of the Pagan clergy, to do so?

6. No one should cast spells or throw magic around to threaten

people, to make themselves look important and powerful, or to make fun of the practice of magic itself. If you do, you do so at your own risk. You can be sure there will be consequences, and you can be sure that you will never see it coming – it will be that swift and devastating.

7.   Magic can be used for personal gain, but it should be used in an honorable fashion. This means that you don't deliberately harm someone to further your own cause, or advance yourself at their expense in any way.

There are people who feel otherwise about this principle, who feel magic should never be used for personal gain, and I would have to disagree with them. Why were we given this power, if not to improve ourselves, make life better, and enrich our existence in order to reach our full potential?

8.   If you have any doubt that magic will work – it won't.

Remember that magic is pure energy directed through time and space by the force of your will. Nothing can kill magic faster than doubt. This is another reason that you do not speak of your spell casting to anyone. Their doubt and skepticism, or ridicule, is also energy; and it will move with lightning speed to smother your magic.

A Code of Ethics for the Gray Witch

1. Consider carefully all the possible outcomes of a spell, and then expect the unexpected.

This rule, more or less, is telling you not to act rashly, or in anger, but to think things through and try to view circumstances and objectives on a level plane.

And yet, because we are mere mortals, don't be surprised to discover that you may not have thought of every possible scenario. Magic is pure energy, not an intelligent entity. This energy will move quickly through the path of least resistance.

* * *

Does this mean the witch hovers in nail-biting hesitation because she thinks there may be some possible fallout from a prospective spell that she hasn't thought of? No.

Of course you want your magic to work the way you've intended, but this may not always be the end result, and this could be because a higher power within the universe has a better perspective than you. This higher power acts on this knowledge, setting circumstances into motion that will benefit you, teach you something, protect you, or expose you to something that you would have otherwise avoided.

There is a reason for everything; nothing that happens is by chance, and this includes the final results of the manifestation of our magic.

2. Choose carefully your confidants, that their loyalty is strong and their friendship pure.

Only confide in those you know, without a doubt, can be trusted to keep secrets. If someone you consider a close friend and confidant ever betrays your trust, know that they may do it again, having done it once.

Beware of those who seek your friendship only to further themselves through association. Once they feel they have their feet firmly planted on the ladder to success and recognition, they may reach out and kick you square in the face.

Beware of enemies who come to you in the guise of friends. They only wish to learn your secrets in order to destroy you from within.

* * *

If you think that the Pagan world and its inhabitants come from a 'higher plane' and are somehow exempt from earthy, downright dirty mortal behavior, guess again. I've seen just as much back-stabbing and petty immature whining from a Pagan as I have from someone on any other spiritual path. And when the Pagan acts in this way, they try just as hard to justify their bad behavior.

We're all human...and you have to be just as careful who you choose for a friend or confidant in the Pagan world as you would anywhere else. Egos seem to run high among occult practitioners. Everyone has an opinion, everyone wants to be taken seriously (who wouldn't?), and sometimes you may meet someone who tries to get ahead in the world by stepping on those closest to them.

You may also run into charlatans in the magical world who try to take advantage of your belief in the supernatural and the occult. Don't stop believing in or practicing your magic, but learn to recognize those who may misuse it.

3. *'A witch who cannot hex cannot heal'...but be able to discern when this energy is needed and when it is desired.*

Yes, the gray witch may throw a hex once in a while, but there will be good cause and serious thought put into it. It is not something done lightly or often.

Her power is not stagnant. The witch does not fear stepping into the shadows in order to grab the dark energy found there, for the gray witch knows that balance must be kept in all things, including the energies she uses.

The gray witch embraces the light and the dark aspects of her being, knowing she must use wisdom and discretion in the use of both.

It is an awesome responsibility.

* * *

Most of the Pagans today come from backgrounds steeped in the Judeo-Christian paths, and there is a completely different mindset to so many things in the world of the witch – and especially the world of the gray witch. I so often see the effects of a Christian upbringing in the views, decisions, and practices of modern-day Pagans. I'm not saying that this is altogether a bad thing – lumping it all into one negative black ball; but so often, this mindset – which was created to control – is still controlling the thought processes and actions of the modern-day witch and Pagan. And this puts her at a grave disadvantage, virtually shackling her in a figurative way to the pillory post or the burning stake.

Quite frankly, what is not acceptable in the practice of Christianity or Judaism is often very acceptable to the witch...and this includes revenge and retribution aimed at our enemies in the form of a hex or curse.

4. Beware of casting a spell against one of your own kind; remember that she has the power and the knowledge to retaliate.

Casting a negative spell against a sister witch may lead to a 'Witch War'. This gives us a visual of powerful women, squared off beneath a dark sky, throwing lightning bolts at one another. The reality is more like two immature children, feet stubbornly planted, pouty faces in place, taking turns slapping each other's cheek.

The witches among us all know that there are spells to break another witch's spell, and spells that will even throw the negative energy a witch has cast back upon her.

Remember to always seek wisdom, maturity, and restraint. Above all else, aspire to dignity.

* * *

In a world strongly influenced by Christianity as well as Judaism and other mainstream religions, why on earth would we want to fight with our own kind? This not only makes the witch and Pagan look ridiculous and hypocritical; it also weakens the cause of Paganism for the rest of the occult-practicing population.

There are enough social issues faced by the witch practitioner without having to worry about watching our back with one of our own. And what witch in her right mind would dare cast negative magic on another witch? You don't have to be a rocket scientist to figure out that it isn't going to work – and if it does, the victim in this scenario might just throw back enough retribution to bury the perpetrator up to her eyeballs in her own negative energy.

Get along – swallow your pride, sit on your tongue, 'agree to disagree', or whatever else it takes. Pagans, and witches in particular, are going to benefit by facing the rest of the world as a united front.

5. Be of sound sane logic when deciding to cast any spell. Give your magic power and strength by adding to it a healthy dose of purpose and integrity.

Symbols of Witchcraft

The Triangle of Manifestation
You will find in the practice of witchcraft that numbers, symbols, and physics all come together to create magic, to allow the physical manifestation of a thought, a wish, or a desire into the physical realm of our mundane world. One of these symbols is the triangle, a shape made up of three sides, the number '3' holding a special meaning to the witch.

There are 'three' faces, or aspects, to the Goddess, as well as the God. Spells are cast 'by the power of three times three'. Herbs and other ingredients are often added to spells in 'threes', and so it goes. Three is a number filled with power and the promise of magic.

In the case of the Triangle of Manifestation the three sides of the triangle represent:

1. Time
2. Space
3. Energy

Time: 'When' you cast a spell is as important as 'what' you cast a spell with, and there are magical correspondences that involve particular energies for certain days of the week; astrological correspondences pertaining to planetary influences; as well as that all-important, ever-present, moon phase. You'll find more information on these correspondences coming up, and you may very well find this to be the most used information in this book.

Space: You must have a space in which to work, a special place to light your candles, chant your chants, invoke your God or Goddess, burn your written spells, and dance your dance.

This special place will most likely be a magic circle – no matter the location you choose to cast your spells or perform your rituals, whether it's a picturesque wooded glade or the middle of your living room.

The magic circle is sacred space that you create with special words and actions. It is a safe haven in which to work magic and perform rituals. It is as impenetrable to negative or evil energies as the most fantastic cathedral or the quaintest country church.

You'll find all the information you'll need to create a magic circle in the ritual section of this book.

Energy: You must raise energy to cast a spell. Without it your spell cannot manifest; in fact, it will not exist.

You can raise energy in many ways: by drumming, dancing, chanting, and occasionally I've noticed that just the excitement and anticipation of casting a spell causes a natural rush of adrenaline that adds to these methods in a surprising and potent display of good old-fashioned foot-stompin' magic.

Time + Space + Energy = Manifestation of Your Spell

Just as numbers and symbols are used in the practice of witchcraft to create magic, there are special gestures that may be used as well. In the practice of ritual magic there is a hand gesture that brings to life the Triangle of Manifestation.

Hold your hands before you, fingers held together, your thumbs spread. Bring together the tips of your thumbs and the tips of your index fingers.

Voilà, you have just created the Triangle of Manifestation. Now peer through the center of this magical symbol and bring to life your magic.

The Witches' Pyramid

As long as we're working with the power of '3', there is yet another symbol, another geometric shape, used to illustrate and pinpoint what is needed to cast successful magic spells.

It is the pyramid – the Witches' Pyramid. This symbolic shape and image represents:

1. Imagination
2. Will
3. Visualization

In the end, beyond physical props used by the witch to cast spells – incense, candles, herbs, pieces of thread, ribbon, nails, bones and stones, poppets and potions – magic is created by the witch's mind.

The props are just a cue, a crutch, to help us focus, to trigger our subconscious, to remove us mentally and spiritually from the everyday mundane world, to help us step above it and reach towards the etheric plane – where magic is possible.

The Triangle of Manifestation can be used as the framework for the Witches' Pyramid. The framework must be set in place first to produce a solid foundation. After this is accomplished, we can begin to construct the walls.

The first wall of the Witches' Pyramid:

Imagination

How lively is yours? Can you imagine changing the circumstances of your life? A better job, larger house, safer vehicle, harmony where there is discord, partnership where there is solitude, safety where there is danger, etc.

Do you daydream unique scenarios?

In order to bring about change, using magic, you have to be able to imagine what life would be like with those changes already in place.

The second wall of the Witches' Pyramid:

Will

How strong is yours? Once your mind is made up, is it easily changed? When you want something, do you get it? Are you determined? Stubborn?

Your will provides the fuel for your spell. The strength of your will determines how far it shall go. The power of your determination explodes into magical manifestation.

It becomes an 'Aha!' moment across the universe.

The third wall of the Witches' Pyramid:

Visualization

How realistic is yours? Can you close your eyes right now and feel a banana in your left hand? Can you see it in your mind, as clearly as if it were really there? Can you reach with your right hand, grasp the rough stem of this banana, snap it, and peel it away? Can you hear the sound of the stem snapping? Can you smell the banana as you peel away the skin?

Now can you do this all over again – with your eyes open?

What you wish to manifest with your spell must be so real to you it is as if it already exists. If you cannot create it within your mind's eye, you cannot manifest it within the physical world.

Imagination + Will + Visualization = Manifestation of Your Spell

The Heptagram

The heptagram is a seven-pointed star. Each point represents a planet, and beginning with the top point moving clockwise, this includes: Saturn, Jupiter, Mars, the Sun, Venus, Mercury, and the Moon. This symbol can be found in old grimoires and represents the movement and speed of the planets through the heavens, as well as the celestial energies of the seven days of the week.

This symbol can be used to invoke the energies of the planets, or the energy of a particular planet you need for your spell crafting, in many ways: trace this symbol on your spell candles; highlight the energy of a particular planet by decorating an altar with those things that correspond to its energy, and include the heptagram to reinforce it; use it in mojo bags and on talismans.

The Triple Ring

This trinity symbol originated with the Celts. The triple ring is also called the triquetra and can be traced back as far as 600 CE (Common Era). Throughout the Celtic tradition, the symbol of the trinity and the significance of the number '3' can be found in their mythology and belief system. There are the three faces of the Goddess – Maiden, Mother, and Crone; the three faces of the God – Green Man, Horned God, and Sage; witches often cast a triple circle around their sacred space; spells are chanted three times; and so it goes. The Celtic knot also represents three planes of existence: the body, mind, and spirit.

The essence of this symbol is three elements with no beginning and no end...the power of three, eternally.

The Triceps

The symbol of the triceps was often found in Druidic traditions and was used to invoke the powers of Earth – land, sky, and sea.

It can be used as a symbol of protection and in spells for prosperity.

The triceps is actually a cut-away triangle formed of three diamonds or 'othala' runes and is a less common version of the Valknut – three interlocking complete triangles found in the Norse traditions.

The Valknut is symbolic and suggestive of related Celtic symbols of motherhood/rebirth, perhaps a triple goddess symbol at some point, the nine points representative of pregnancy and reincarnation, and the nine worlds (nine fates) of Norse mythology.

Elixir of the Moon

This beautiful symbol was designed in the 15th century and is a model of our solar system, keeping the sun and moon at the center, as would have been the popular belief in the Middle Ages. The symbols for the planets ring the outside: Mercury, Venus, Mars, Saturn, and Jupiter.

And oddly enough, there are three spaces available for the three planets that were not yet discovered at the time this symbol was created. Coincidence? Synchronicity? Whatever it is, I love it when incidents like this occur.

I have painted a large stone with the Elixir of the Moon, and I use this talisman to invoke the energy of all the planets, or a particular energy that may be needed for my spell work: Mercury for spells involving communication, mental endeavors, and those things of the mind; Venus for love and beauty, relationships, and the arts; Mars for defense, strength, spells calling for powerful no-nonsense energy; Saturn for the dark side, hexes, breaking a curse, dispersing negative energy; Jupiter for expansion, financial and legal matters, spells that involve details of the business side of life.

The Symbol for Alchemy

Alchemy brings to mind the image of ancient sorcerers bent over their tables of bottles, jars, potions, and candle flames, attempting to change lead into gold; seeking the philosopher's stone; and opening doorways between science and magic.

And yes, there is a symbol for alchemy: a circle within a square, within a triangle, within a circle – this description is from the inside out. Looking at this symbol from the outside working inward, we see that the first circle represents the void; the triangle – thought activation, by will and intention; the square – the influence of deity upon the process of magic; and the inner circle – manifestation into the physical world.

This is magic.

Alchemy could be explained as 'the science of magic', for it is a science. It is the study of 'esoteric' (secret) knowledge that uses different natural abilities – such as visualization and will-power; along with natural components – herbs, stones, and other physical items; as well as the energy of a deity or spirit, to produce a physical manifestation into our world of solid matter.

This manifestation can be either something of a physical nature, or a chain of desired circumstances.

Color Correspondences for Alchemy

Black: chaos

Red: information and change

White: purification

Gold: transformation

Alchemical Chant for Spell Work

'From the black of empty space,

To red of action,

I do embrace

Pure white of cleansing power,

Transform to gold,

Upon this hour.'

Use this chant to conjure physical manifestations of your spell work. As you recite these words, visualize your intentions moving from the black void – pulling it out of the etheric plane, to the red of action – churning with movement and energy, through the cleansing of white – purifying your intentions, and finally to gold – or the physical manifestation and realization of your will.

The Hermetic Quaternary

To Know
To Dare
To Will
To Keep Silent

The Hermetic Quaternary, also known as the 'Four Laws of the Magus' or 'The Witches' Ladder', is traditionally attributed to Hermes Trismegistus. These laws are associated with ceremonial magic and believed to have originated in ancient Egypt. Although associated with ceremonial magic, these axioms are as relevant to the cottage witch as they are to the highest ceremonial magician. Embrace them.

The longer you delve into the study of the occult and the more information and knowledge you uncover, the more you will come to realize that everything is interconnected. And so it is with the Hermetic Quaternary. You will find that each of these four laws is represented by one of the four elements:

Air = To Know
Water = To Dare
Fire = To Will
Earth = To Keep Silent

To Know:

Knowledge is power. And on this, the first rung of what I call

'The Witches' Ladder', we concentrate on learning the secrets, discovering the answers, absorbing as much information as we can in order to become what we know we are and to practice the magic that has always been part of our destiny.

To Dare:
The second rung upon the Witches' Ladder declares our strong spirit and our determination to learn the ancient ways and incorporate them into our daily lives. We challenge the 'norms' of our society and culture and proudly walk the way of witch. We do the magic.

To Will:
This axiom means that the witch's will is strong enough to manifest her wishes and desires into the physical world. It's not a matter of helter-skelter determination; but a disciplined, knowledgeable, organized use of 'mind over matter'.

To Keep Silent:
This is perhaps the most important rung upon the Witches' Ladder, so much so that I began this book with it, along with an explanation of the meaning and the consequences that would result if it were ignored. The last rung on the Witches' Ladder tells us to guard the energy of our spells, the secrets of our coven, and the safety of our fellow witches by maintaining silence.

As with so many concepts in witchcraft, the Hermetic Quaternary is represented by a very specific symbol: a triangle within a circle.

'To Know' is the base of the triangle, for without knowledge there is no foundation. 'To Dare' is the left wall of the triangle, 'To Will' the right wall, for upon these all magic and power is built. 'To Keep Silent' overrides it all, the sacred circle protecting the witch and everything she stands for in her endeavor to live a magical life with dignity, grace, and fortitude.

The symbolism continues...

The Pentagram

Each of the axioms of the Witches' Ladder, along with their corresponding elements, have a place upon the pentagram – the beautiful, and much maligned, five-pointed star that has come to symbolize the witch, perhaps more than any other image.

'To Know = Air' lies at the upper right point of the star; 'To Will = Fire' can be found at the lower left point; 'To Dare = Water' is the upper left point; 'To Keep Silent = Earth' can be found at the lower right point.

And the top point of the pentagram? This point represents Spirit; and to each individual this may be something different – the Goddess or the God (or both), a universal intelligence, a supreme being, the All, the Source, etc.

The witch will know, without a doubt, what it means to her.

The Elements

The four natural elements – earth, air, fire, and water – are used in the practice of witchcraft, both to call upon their energies and corresponding entities for casting spells; for protection – to guard the magic circle; for rituals of religious observance; for the movement of specific energies within your living space in an effort to cleanse/empower that space; and for their individual connection to specific stones and herbs used for a myriad magical intentions. The uses for the elements in a witch's magical and spiritual practice are as varied and numerous as there are witches to use them.

The Eastern tradition, it should at least be noted, has five elements: wood, fire, metal, water, and earth. For the intentions of this book, a publication of my personal Book of Shadows, and in view of my own practice – that which combines Celtic traditions, European witchcraft, and hoodoo – we're only going to deal with the four classic elements.

The correspondences for these elements are very specific and quite detailed. Their energy, and thus their temperament, or that of the entities associated with each element, is also very personal, very real, and very powerful.

These elements should be respected and used properly. In trying to think of a comparison on this topic, the Christian entity of the Holy Ghost comes to mind – it is a spirit both revered and respected, and sometimes even feared, by the practitioners of Christianity. It is with the same demeanor, one of respect and reverence, that the witch views the elements.

So it is with a healthy dose of awe and caution that the witch approaches and invokes the four elements. The experienced magical practitioner realizes the power behind these energies/entities, and although I would not say the witch fears the elements, she is wise enough not to toy with them.

Earth

Earth is all the treasures buried deep within the soul. It is the material things you long for and were told you shouldn't have. It is the security of that which is solid and immovable, and it is 'manifestation' into the real world of touch and taste, smell and sight.

Energy: feminine/receptive
Correspondences for Earth
Direction: north
Color: green
Elemental: gnomes
Season: winter
Time of Day: midnight
Ritual Tools: pentacles and salt
Tarot: pentacles
Zodiac: Taurus, Virgo, Capricorn
Angel: Uriel
Hermetic Axiom: 'To Know'

Zodiac: Taurus, Virgo, Capricorn

Invoking/Banishing Pentagrams:

Earth Energy

You will use the energy of Earth when you wish to manifest those things in your life that smack of the material – money, possessions, or changes of circumstances in life that will lead to the acquisition of these things.

Where the cry of Christianity proclaims that a saintly pursuit of poverty and a spartan lifestyle leads to spiritual fulfillment and enlightenment, the witch knows that she was put upon this earth to experience all of it to the best of her ability, to enjoy that which surrounds her, to obtain that which she deserves, to wallow in the miracle of the physical world.

The witch indulges herself with no trace of Christian guilt, for she knows she is 'of the earth', and so she freely uses the natural energy of this element.

Using 'Earth' in Spells

You can incorporate the use of the element Earth in your spells by burying the remnants of your spell work (candle wax, ashes, ribbons, poppets, bottles, etc.) in the earth itself – on your property for positive receptive magic and off your property for negative projective magic.

You can place a symbol of the pentacle on or near your front door for protection. Wear a silver pentacle pendant for protection, as well as for a sign of devotion to your religion and your god/goddess; or wear a stone aligned with the energy of Earth for a particular intention.

Leave a bowl of salt on your nightstand to keep away spirits and get a restful night's sleep; leave a bowl of stones or river rocks sitting on the coffee table to help ground the atmosphere of the room, or dispel giddy energy from guests.

Place the image of a gnome in your garden, and leave the offering of a silver coin beneath him to insure prosperity. Place the Earth sigil upon those things you wish to protect: on your front door, to protect all within; on a stone talisman placed in your vehicle for safe travel; or over the top of a written spell to physically manifest that which you desire.

Air

Air is the soft breeze on your face that makes you feel touched and not touched. It is thought brought alive and moved through space and time by the Divine. Air is the part of your mind that is clear and sharp and focused and ever changing, never still and never content, but always swept up within another breeze and moved along on the current of time.

Energy: masculine/projective
Correspondences for Air
Direction: east
Color: yellow
Elemental: sylphs and fairies
Season: spring
Time of Day: dawn
Ritual Tools: athame, sword
Tarot: swords
Angel: Raphael
Hermetic Axiom: 'To Will'
Zodiac: Libra, Aquarius, Gemini

Invoking/Banishing Pentagrams:

Air Energy

Where Earth energy envelops the physical, Air energy is purely mental. It encompasses that which cannot be seen, but which makes us who we are and gives substance to our existence – our intelligence, mentality, our ideas that lead to creativity, our assumptions, thoughts, and spark of genius. All of this and more stems from the element of Air.

Air, the element, touches us whenever we pursue knowledge, seek answers, ponder the universe and our place in it, when we write, draw, paint, and compose. Because of the element of Air, within all of future humanity there resides unwritten novels, unpainted masterpieces, sculpture, music, medical discoveries, inventions, and creations as yet unperceived and unrealized.

And when the elements dance their dance, when Air mingles with Earth, all of these wonderful things will be given a pathway into the physical world.

Using 'Air' in Spells

You can harness the power and potential of Air when you are absorbed in important mental endeavors, such as the student facing tests: burn a yellow candle at your desk while you study; tuck an herb aligned with Air energy in the back of your book; carry with you to your exams a small bag filled with stones and herbs corresponding to Air, as well as your intentions of a good grade.

Air energy is used in communication; it is the essence of thought to thought, mind to mind. Send a magical message by writing it upon a piece of paper and tying it with a yellow ribbon to a tree, the back porch roof, a fence post, etc., and allow the natural winds of Air to send this message on its way.

When you are composing, writing, creating, light your favorite incense to fill your work space with the energy of Air and entice your muse to sit upon your shoulder and whisper in your ear.

Fire

Fire is that physical passion so burning that it can consume. It is enthusiasm so powerful that it is what drives you to succeed. Fire is that fiery will that doesn't allow you to give up in the face of adversity. It is what draws lovers together across insurmountable odds and provokes the passion that fights endlessly for justice.

Energy: masculine/projective
Correspondences for Fire
Direction: south
Color: red
Elemental: salamanders
Season: summer
Time of Day: midday
Ritual tools: candle, wand, staff
Tarot: wands
Angel: Michael
Hermetic Axiom: 'To Dare'
Zodiac: Aries, Leo, Sagittarius

Invoking/Banishing Pentagrams:

Fire Energy

You will use the energy of Fire when you want to incite fiery passion into any project, relationship, spell, or cause.

Fire is the heat of lust, burning desire made visible, flaming persistent unrelenting will-power; but beware, because Fire is also the great destroyer. The element of Fire purges our intentions, our actions, our hidden agendas with an unforgiving heat, leaving the landscape black and bare so that we can begin to rebuild our path, our life, our world, and our psyche.

Use the energy of Fire with caution, with purpose, with determination; and never take your eyes off it, for if you do, you may suddenly feel its flames licking at your soul.

Using 'Fire' in Spells

You will use the energy of Fire to rekindle dwindling passion or begin the heat of new desire by carving your name and the name of your beloved on a red candle. In the flame of this candle burn a paper on which you've poured out your heart.

Fire will be used in a wide variety of candle magic, in conjunction with the other elements, adding its fiery will to all intentions.

Use Fire to consume all of the materials – paper, poppets, personal items, images – which you have used to cast a spell. Then allow the ashes from the flames to mingle with the winds of Air – for one feeds into the other.

Toss the ashes into the wind, and feel the movement of magical energy.

Water

Water is the mist of yesterday, today and tomorrow all wrapped up into one magical moment. Water is dreams and visions and questing endlessly to know the unknown. It is divination – searching for answers and listening to the universe for its response. It is the mystical and the elusive. It slips through your fingers leaving you wet and cold and shivering, knowing that you have been touched by the Divine.

Energy: feminine/receptive
Correspondences for Water
Direction: west
Color: blue
Elemental: undines
Season: autumn
Time of Day: sunset
Ritual Tools: chalice and cauldron
Tarot: cups
Angel: Gabriel
Hermetic Axiom: 'To Keep Silent'
Zodiac: Cancer, Scorpio, Pisces

Water Energy

You will use the energy of Water when you float through your dreams, swim through your emotions and wade through your sense of intuition.

The energy of Water is fluid, always moving, ever changing, sometimes calm and other times rolling and crashing as wild as the ocean waves.

Water is the supreme symbol of the feminine, of the Mother Goddess, of the womb, of rebirth and regeneration. It is crystal clear and glistening in the sunlight, revealing everything before you; or it is dark and murky, hiding that which you are not ready to see, or that which you must find on your own. The element of Water highlights visions, psychism, dreams, and the mystical.

Using 'Water' in Spells

Water will be used to cleanse and purify the space you will make sacred for your spell casting and rituals. Drop a pinch of salt in a small bowl of water and, using your fingers or a sprig of sage or rosemary, sprinkle (asperge) the area where you will cast your magic circle.

The power of Water will be used in spells for dreams – create a dream bag to place beneath your pillow using herbs and stones aligned with the energy of Water. Make use of the morning dew for spells of beauty and youth; it's a magical elixir prepared by nature and presented to you in reverence and purity at the dawn of each new day.

You will use the energy of Water to strengthen your intuition, to call on the power of the Goddess, to awaken the psychic side of yourself, and to cleanse and purify your surroundings, your body, and your intentions.

Thirteen Powers of the Witch

1. To curse
2. To bless
3. To conjure
4. To communicate with spirits
5. To communicate with animals
6. To control the winds
7. To heal
8. To divine the future
9. To give wise counsel
10. To know the energies of the herbs
11. To know the energies of the stones
12. To shape-shift
13. To see visions

The powers and gifts a witch develops, both from her studies and from her natural abilities, will be varied, individualistic, and supremely unique to each witch. Not everyone will excel at all the powers. Most witches discover they have a special talent or affinity for one or two particular powers, which can be honed and strengthened with hard work and diligence.

The Witches' Alphabet

The Witches' Alphabet, or 'Theban Script', is believed to have been created during the Middle Ages by the magician Honorius the Theban.

Secret codes or alphabets have long been used by secret societies, groups, covens, and clans. The use of such an alphabet lends a certain air of mystery, insures secrecy, as it is usually only revealed to initiates, and adds power to the words created.

This alphabet can be used by the modern-day witch when she writes out her spells on parchment, carves names and intentions in spell candles, or sends a special message to her coven or a fellow witch.

The use of this alphabet may seem difficult at first, but with patience and practice it becomes easier, and your proficiency in its use will grow.

It must be noted: I don't advise anyone to create a huge Book of Shadows, or any other large chunk of material, exclusively in this or any other code or secret alphabet. Personally, I find using the Witches' Alphabet in this way clumsy and difficult; not to mention that someday, when your book is passed down, the recipient may not be familiar with this secret alphabet and the translation of your work would be arduous.

I prefer to use the Witches' Alphabet exclusively for spell work or special secret messages.

Initiation

Those witches joining a coven may find themselves facing a three-year course of study which will take them through the 'three degrees'. These degrees are a progression of levels within the hierarchy of a coven, from the first-degree witch passing through her period as a novice, to the third-degree witch who will carry more responsibility within the group – having a hand in making decisions, planning rituals, mentoring students, etc. The prescribed length of time to work your way through each degree is traditionally 'a year and a day'.

It should be noted that no matter how many titles a witch might have, no matter how impressive her accomplishments, the study of witchcraft is an ongoing lifelong process. The expansion of knowledge and power, the techniques and art of spell crafting, as well as the development of personal gifts are not something that is completed before an initiation, nor does the process stop after initiation. Once you begin this quest, you will find that it is a journey that lasts a lifetime, perhaps several lifetimes.

What about the solitary witch – can she initiate herself?

You bet your sweet cauldron she can.

There is a lot of debate upon this topic in the Wiccan world. There is controversy and arguments; there is foot stomping, shouting, and lines drawn in the sand. And when the storm cloud dissipates and the air clears, the ultimate answer is – you can do whatever the hell you want to do on this point. There are no Wiccan storm troopers who are going to burst into your sacred space and halt your self-initiation ritual.

Initiation in itself is a rite of passage, a very personal rite of passage, that every Pagan will experience in their own time and on their own terms. You will know when you are going through a rite of passage; you won't need someone standing over you with a checklist, squinting their eyes as they appraise you, measuring you to their own personal yardstick of witchery.

Modern witchcraft has only been stumbling around in our modern world since Gerald Gardner penciled his thoughts, spells, insights, and personal formulas on the subject in his notebooks during the 1950s. Before that, we have to retreat back into the dark days of the Middle Ages, back to the Burning Times, the Inquisition, when women were tortured and put to death for practicing witchcraft. Knowledge that was passed down verbally was lost forever through this slaughter of individuals. So much knowledge was lost, in fact, that what we practice today are but bits and pieces of what once was. I don't know how anyone can proclaim today that this or that was done a particular way, this or that was accepted or frowned upon. Much of what so many of the experts in these modern times tell us with such authority and finality is mere speculation.

I like to think that the belly of witchcraft, the very center of it, lies in the solitary old woman who lived quietly in her cottage at the edge of the village, the cottage most people avoided and skirted around, until they found themselves compelled to sneak through the shadows of night and knock on her door – seeking herbs for an illness, help with a baby's birth, or magic to solve a problem.

Over the course of witchcraft's modern history, a few people, many of them men, have tried to structure this ancient practice, to corral it, control it, give it rules and regulations somewhat simulating the structure of Christian churches. When in fact the essence of witchcraft is formless – free-spirited, constantly mutating, lending its magic to the world, whether the bulk of the world and its inhabitants are aware of it or not.

I don't believe that witchcraft can be defined. There is absolute truth in the statement that there are as many different ways of practicing witchcraft as there are witches to practice it.

Although I belong to a coven now, I began my journey on the witches' path alone, and I stayed upon a solitary course for many years. I have also experienced a formal solitary initiation through ritual; and I found it to be one of the most memorable and moving experiences of my life. And to the surprise and wonder of many, I experienced self-initiation – complete with formal rituals – to the third degree. I chose to mark my personal solitary journey through the Craft with a formal ritual at each point. I encourage others to do the same.

Although I am a member of a coven now and cherish my sisters, I have always – and will always – describe myself as a third-degree, self-initiated, solitary witch, a rebel on this path of the wild-woman.

Understand that *you will* experience the three degrees of inward initiation, whether you choose to formally recognize it, or to outwardly celebrate and acknowledge it. I chose to whole-heartedly celebrate and honor these initiations with ritual.

And what are the 'three degrees'? What encompasses this progressive journey?

First Degree
You felt the calling. Something intangible and unnamable whispered in your ear, tugged at your dreams. It eventually became louder, more insistent, and it began to appear in your

everyday life as a series of uniquely synchronistic experiences...a book title leaped out at you when browsing a bookstore; the trees seemed, for an instant, to be speaking to you as the wind passed through their leaves; an animal appeared to you, not once, but several times in several forms – the living raven sitting on your back porch rail, intently staring at you through the windows; the image of the raven, a logo on the side of a vehicle, passing you on the freeway; a statuary image of the raven, inexplicably showing up on a receptionist's desk in the dentist or doctor's office.

Every individual's experience is unique, and at the same time, I've noticed a similarity.

When the pull becomes strong enough and the calling can no longer be ignored, you begin your first year of study, of enlightenment, of growth and development. During this time, unknown planes of existence and new concepts unroll themselves before you. The world, as you know it, disappears and takes on new dimensions, colors, spirit, forms, and infinite possibilities.

At the end of the first year, doors to the universe have been flung open. Armed with this new knowledge, you stand at the threshold of a new life. You realize that you will never be able to retreat to your previous existence, because once you 'know', you can never 'unknow'.

You have reached the first degree.

Second Degree

The second year of study plunges ahead, in an almost frenzied manic attempt to put into action the newly revealed knowledge you have acquired. You are not only going to put into practice all of the information you've absorbed; you're also going to manifest it into your everyday life and the physical world.

You're going to cast circles in space that you yourself have cleansed and prepared. You will cast these circles at first in a quivering voice with trembling hands, marveling at the energy you feel and struck by the stark reality of it all.

You are going to cast spells in the same way, with heightened senses and a rush of adrenaline that adds its natural power to your work. Never again will you feel this rush of energy as you do during this time, the rush of magic enveloped with ethereal intensity. For it is at this time that it finally dawns on you what you are and what you're capable of doing.

When this realization hits you, you will know that you've reached the second degree.

Third Degree

With the third year comes a sense of peace, both from within yourself and from the natural world around you. The second degree was framed so explicitly within physical experiences that it left you with raw pulsating nerve endings throbbing from over-stimulation. But the third year is going to abandon the physical world altogether, leaving it behind, taking you by the hand into a new and profound awareness of the spiritual side of witchcraft.

This is when many of you will discover your personal path, your patron gods or goddesses, your core beliefs, your strengths and your weaknesses. For the first time in your life perhaps, the true meaning of 'Spirit' becomes a concrete reality.

It's at this time that your gifts may begin to surface. For some, psychic ability will awaken and leave you in a state of astounded amazement, eager to strengthen this new occult muscle and put it to good use. For others the miraculous world of herbs may unfold before you in a panorama of colored blossoms, green leaves, dried stems, and dormant magic lying within each gently gathered plant. Whatever your gift or gifts may be, you will recognize your potential once it has been revealed to you.

For each witch this will be an extremely personal journey. And when you feel the power of the universe touching you gently on the shoulder, and you know where your life's work lies...you've reached the third degree.

The Ritual

You will receive numerous informal initiations along your journey on the witches' path, I assure you, and you will feel the magic and power from these spiritually enlightened moments as intensely as you would during the most formal and ceremonial of rituals.

However, when your first year and a day passes, there will be within you a tremendous desire to cement this new path, this new life, with the age-old rite of initiation. You will feel a bond you cannot even explain to yourself with the herbs and stones, gods and goddesses, nature, unseen spirits, and the energy of the elements. It will be as though all of your senses had been shut off from the world your entire life – and now they are open and alive.

You are ready to experience initiation.

(You'll find an initiation ritual in the ritual section of this book.)

Your Craft Name

At birth, your parents named you. They probably did this with care and love, and a great deal of thought. And for your entire life, this name has shaped your personality, lent an air of ambiance to your energy, and identified you to yourself and those around you in many ways, through association.

Upon choosing the path of witch – upon receiving initiation into this new life – you will choose a new name, a magical name, a secret name that will be known only to you and perhaps your coven sisters/brothers. This magical name will only be used within a cast circle; it is the name by which the Goddess/God and ancient spirits and beings will recognize you. Within this name resides power and the ability to invoke and call forth spirits and entities. Within this name magic will be made and spells will be cast.

You will choose this name. Think carefully; take your time.

Ask yourself what types of magical energies, entities, and objects you feel drawn to. What aspects of the natural world call to you? Animals, trees, plants, herbs, stones...

This name will come to you, and when it does, you will know it. You will find it in a dream, hear it on the wind, see it in the branches of a tree, the glimmer of a crystal, or the shape of an animal. Once you've taken this magical name through initiation, your life will change. *They* will be able to find you – the gods/goddesses, the elementals, the angels/daemons, the spirits. When you call, they will come.

The Metaphysical Laws of Witchcraft

1. The Law of Rebound
2. The Law of Requests
3. The Law of Challenge
4. The Law of Equalities
5. The Law of Balance
6. The Law of Summons
7. The Law of Polarities
8. The Law of Cause and Effect
9. The Law of Abundance

I've read several interpretations of these laws. Although informative and often poetic, the majority of these narratives were long-winded and obviously muse-inspired, which is not necessarily a bad thing; but it resulted in beautiful, philosophical, dreamy tangents that left me scratching my head, not quite able to find the point of it all in the end.

For our purpose, as well as clarity, I intend to be brief and to the point.

First off, let me say, the life of the witch is not a wild and unruly existence filled with impulsive behavior, off-the-wall decisions, and no repercussions. On the contrary, being knowledgeable in the world of the occult, having the ability to practice magic and divination, as well as being aware of certain energies and magical possibilities in the world, brings with it tremendous responsibility and repercussions that can be merciless.

The witch is, indeed, solely responsible for her actions, the karma which results, and any fallout which might remain from her magic. The following laws, or rules if you will, help the magical practitioner to police herself, to know where the dangers lie, and to know what to expect from various magical practices and energies.

1. The Law of Rebound
'What goes around comes around' pretty much exemplifies the first law and is often embraced by Wiccans, who believe that what you send out comes back three times greater, or 'three times three' – be it good or bad, dark or light. And let me clarify here that 'good' means good, and 'dark' means simply a different shade of energy than light.

My grandmother pretty much lived by this motto her entire life without realizing the significance of it from an occult perspective. She always told me: 'Don't wish anything bad on someone, because it will come back on you.' And her instinctual understanding of this basic metaphysical rule helped her to build her own life's path. Her emphatic acknowledgment of and faith in this premise made a lasting impact upon me.

Does this mean that you will never pull any magical punches? Of course not. You'll know when to flex your magical muscle; and you'll know when to flex it in tune with karma, not against it.

2. The Law of Requests
In the casting of spells, the spell is repeated three times – and there's that magic number again. The number '3' holds a certain power

and innate magic in it that carries forth in a variety of circumstances: there are three phases to the God and Goddess,
generally three phases of initiation, a combination of at least
three herbs are used in most spells, the witches' circle is cast
three times round, and so it goes. Have you ever wondered why
very important documents are usually printed out in triplicate?

Three is a power number, a magical number, a number of
mystery and purpose. Repeat your spells three times and feel the
power and magic build with each repetition.

3. The Law of Challenge

Question that which seems illogical or suspicious, that which
rings your psychic doorbell and activates that little voice in your
head. Assume nothing, whether it be a spirit, a vision, or
anything else. Just because it looks like an angel doesn't mean it
is an angel.

This law reminds me for some reason of Ouija boards and the
fact that you don't take everything a spirit tells you through this
medium at face value; because really, do you honestly know to
what or whom you're speaking? The same thing goes for
invoking spirits, gods/goddesses, or any other entity. If it doesn't
'feel' right, it probably isn't, and don't be afraid to challenge it,
banish it, or dispel it if need be.

This law makes me think of some religions that teach blind
unquestioned obedience from their members – witchcraft is not
one of those religions. You've got a mind and a brain, and you're
probably wallowing in common sense. Don't be afraid to use it in
order to question that which you find suspicious.

4. The Law of Equalities

When two equal forces connect or converge or impact, one of
these forces will absorb a greater share of the energy generated.
If you took high school physics, this comes as nothing new. And
if you thought that high school physics couldn't possibly have

anything to do with the world of magic or witchcraft, guess again.

The first scenario that comes to mind with this law is warring witches, magical practitioners who are tossing negative energies and spells back and forth upon each other. This energy, this magic, is going to hit head-on – and someone will come out stronger, while the other participant is weakened by the encounter.

This law can also be taken into consideration when determining what magical course is open when there is a situation that needs clarification and action to remedy an imbalance in energy.

5. The Law of Balance

'Moderation in all things' is the warning to be heeded by this law. And Sister Loretta would be proud of me, because this was one of her favorite quotes. Little did this nun know in what context I would be using it some forty years later.

For the best optimum advantage in life, you must maintain a balance, and this doesn't include just the physical world, but the world of body, mind, and spirit.

By body – balance in exercise, diet, rest, and recreation.

By mind – balance in mental activity and work as well as a time to dream.

By spirit – balance in rituals, the four elements, shadow and light, questing and enlightenment.

6. The Law of Summons

Be careful what energies you invoke, and never call up anything you cannot send away. In other words, don't play with fire.

What often leads to unfortunate incidents is inexperience. You have to not only learn your craft thoroughly, but at some point you have to stop talking about it and start doing it. 'Practice makes perfect', so the old saying goes.

One thing that seems to be a cause for unfortunate experiences is when a witch tries to take on a great big ritual filled with entities and energies she is not used to working with, or has never worked with. If you barely know how to cast a circle, you're certainly not ready to invoke Kalima in ritual.

First rule of thumb: know how to set up secure sacred space, how to protect yourself from the influence of unwanted or malevolent energies. Practice, practice, practice – and then be careful as hell when invoking anything. There are people who do not believe that these energies and entities are real. Those people would be wrong.

7. The Law of Polarities

'Opposites attract', it's as simple as that, and take this into consideration when working with magical energy.

Balance projective energy with receptive energy. To cast a spell directed toward the masculine, apply feminine aspects to it and vice versa. This will also apply to working with the elements – balance Water to Earth...Air to Fire – and this can include a variety of combinations, depending on what kind of magic you are doing.

It makes sense really. Take the weather for example. To alleviate a draught, you would use herbs, stones, and items connected to water. And this theory works not just for wet and dry, but hot and cold, dark and light, rich and poor, healthy and ill, strong and weak, etc.

8. The Law of Cause and Effect

'For every action there is a reaction', so think carefully about unexpected repercussions or irresponsibly directed energy. And, by the way, we're back to physics here. I also might add that this law and the first law – the Law of Rebound – share some similarities.

The Law of Cause and Effect is wider and impacts more than the Law of Rebound, which only comes back upon the practitioner. In this circumstance, energies that you unwittingly set loose during inept magical practices can have widespread effects upon the world, nature, specific locations, groups of people, individuals, or the universe in general. This sounds so huge, and some might shake their heads, but it *is* huge. You're messing with other people's bodies, space, homes, energies, dreams, and realities.

Consider carefully all the possible outcomes and repercussions from any magical endeavor.

9. The Law of Abundance

'*Like attracts like*', yes, indeed.

This statement is so true within itself that I was almost tempted to leave it at that. But I won't.

An old saying comes to mind: 'You need money to make money.' This statement is so true and plays in beautifully with the Law of Abundance. In money spells, money is used. It's kept close at hand; your purse should never be without it, your mojo bag should be filled with it – coins, paper money…pennies, nickels, dimes. 'The rich get richer', because they use money to make money – like attracts like.

This theory applies to everything, not just money or material abundance. If you want order and balance in your life, then you must surround yourself with order and balance, projecting these attributes; mirror it in your home and surroundings – even if you don't feel it inside. Imperceptibly at first, it will come to you.

Power Words

'Sticks and stones may break my bones, but words will never hurt me.' Whoever coined this quaint phrase obviously was not aware of the power contained in words. Think about it: words bring people together in love and create harmony, but words also have the power to ignite controversy and conflict.

The witch understands the extraordinary power contained in

words – both the spoken word and the written word. And she incorporates this magic in her spell casting, in hexing and magical modes of protection, usually in rhyme, and always with will and determination.

This is why it is imperative to word your spells carefully, to be precise and exacting in what you're trying to manifest, or what circumstances you are going to change – and include how, when, why.

However, this doesn't mean that you should be frozen with fear when it comes to writing out your spells. When you get to the point where you are ready to perform magic to manifest your desires or change your circumstances, the right words will come to you.

There are a few distinct phrases that stand out, one or two that have even become familiar in mainstream society, mostly mimicked in witchy-flavored movies, and spread by gothy enthusiastic teens.

Among the most popular are:

'So Mote It Be'
This means 'it must be'; not maybe, might, or pretty please. This phrase is spoken in the course of spell casting to seal the deal, to send off the energy in a surge of show and power, to reaffirm that your magic is on its way and manifestation is right around the corner.

The initials to this phrase also carry power and can be written across your spell, carved into spell candles, and used on anything else you want to affirm as a done deal.

'As Above, So Below'
This phrase is spoken after you've cast your circle. It acknowlededges the power of Father Sky and Mother Earth, of the God and the Goddess, the powers above and the powers below. This phrase lets the universe know that the sacred space you've

created is sealed and safe, both protecting you from above and shielding you from below.

The boundaries of this perfect sphere (for that is what a magic circle is – not a one-dimensional circle upon the ground, but a three-dimensional ball of sacred space) will contain the magical energy you raise until you send it off. This magical boundary will also protect you from unwanted or disruptive negative energies or entities…as above, so below.

'Blessed Be'

This is perhaps one of the most popular and most recognized phrases to seep out of the occult world into mainstream culture. It is a blessing, plain and simple. When spoken out loud, or used as the closing in written correspondence, it simply means that you bestow blessings, positive energy, and good wishes upon the recipient. Another form of this phrase, one which seems to be very popular among witches, is 'Bright Blessings'.

'Merry Meet, Merry Part'

This is used as both a greeting and a farewell, a witches' greeting, a Wiccan farewell. It implies that you come together in peace and good will, and at the end of your visit, you shall go your separate ways in peace and good will. It's often followed with the words: 'Till we merry meet again', assuming that you'll still be on friendly terms when you next cross paths.

The witch is the ultimate optimist.

Tools of the Trade

There are a few positively magical items that will be found in every witch's magical cupboard, and I'll be listing those below. But aside from the unusual and exotic tools, you'll need a few everyday mundane items as well, such as plenty of glass jars in various sizes to hold herbs, oils, powders, cat hair, human hair and fingernails, rusty nails, razors, snake sheds, coins, beads, and baubles, etc.

You'll need ribbon in various colors – at least black, for the dark issues, green for money and health, purple for those matters with a psychic bent, white for cleansing, and red for good old love and a little lust.

You'll want paint and paint brushes, chalk, sewing needles and thread – in various colors, as with the ribbon. You'll want a good stock of candles – tea candles, votive candles, pillar candles; at least in all the basic colors, including green, yellow, red, and blue for the elements. You'll want plenty of incense, both stick and cone, as well as ingredients to make your own; you'll want extra candle holders; a variety of small dishes and bowls; strips of material for your altar in an array of colors for holidays, esbats, and spell casting.

You will be amazed at the amount of materials and items you will accumulate when you practice witchcraft.

Below are some of the more unusual items that you'll find invaluable:

The Cauldron

The energy of the cauldron is feminine. The cauldron represents the womb, the Goddess, specifically the Crone. You burn within your cauldron your spell candles, written spells, and herbs. I also use my large cast-iron cauldron to mix magical oils, heating it just until the aroma and the energy of the plants are released.

Your cauldron should be of a convenient size – too small, and it won't hold all your ingredients; too large and it could be too bulky and heavy to lug around, if cast iron. It should certainly be made of a material that is fireproof; and besides cast iron, I have seen a few ceramic cauldrons and some made of brass or copper; although cast iron is the most durable and can take intense heat much better than the latter choices.

I have two cast-iron cauldrons – one is large, and I use this one when I plan to bring out the big guns, when I want to mix up some magical potions and oils, or when I'll be burning a pillar candle over the course of several days; and I have a very small cauldron that's just right for a votive candle, a handful of herbs, and a written spell. The small cauldron is so much easier to lug here or there, when I want to go off to do spells in special locations.

The Athame

This is a witch's ritual knife, usually the size of a dagger, either ornate and expensive, or simple and cheap. My first athame was a black-handled kitchen knife, which I adorned with symbols and braided ribbon. The athame is used to direct energy, particularly when casting a circle, and contrary to popular myth and misrepresentation a witch's athame is never used to physically cut anything.

The Sword

Think 'athame', only bigger. The sword is more ritualistic than the athame, perhaps used on special occasions for esbats and sabbats. I think of it as an accessory with formal dress to complement your ritual robes. But I've also indulged myself with private rituals or spell castings and one of my swords, immersed in the energy. I find swords both beautiful and inspiring, and I've collected several, along with an array of athames. As with the athame, your ritual sword is never used to cut anything; its only purpose is to direct energy, and believe me – it will.

The Bolline

This is a small knife, often with a white handle, though mine is brown wood. This knife is used for practical purposes, such as cutting herbs, carving names and symbols onto spell candles, cutting ribbon or rope, and a hundred other mundane uses that arise in the physical preparations of magic.

The Pentacle

I use this symbol on a trivet upon which I set my cauldron. I made a simple trivet out of a clay tray that's used to hold a flowerpot, turning it upside down, spray-painting it black, and painting a white pentagram in its center. This trivet serves two purposes, the first mundane – it prevents my hot cauldron from burning the surface of whatever I have it sitting on. The second purpose is magical – the power of the pentacle is infused in my spell crafting in this way, the symbol of the elements and Spirit, the symbol of manifestation at its most powerful. I've seen beautiful cast-iron trivets made with the symbol of a pentagram, and a few ceramic trivets that were lovely, but more expensive.

The Mortar and Pestle

The mortar and pestle are used to grind herbs and other ingredients. They come in a variety of colors, can be ceramic or stone, and are often beautiful. I have two – a large set made of banded green onyx that I use when preparing a good-sized batch of herbs for my oils; and a small white porcelain set that I use when grinding ingredients for a spell candle or a mojo bag. It would also be a good idea to have one set to use for poisonous herbs and ingredients.

Magical Correspondences

As I've repeatedly stated, everything is connected. This viewpoint, from an occult perspective, is that the universe can be perceived as one giant spider web. Everything in it, from the smallest stone to a hawk, every plant, individual, and molecule on the face of the earth and beyond, is connected by a thin web of energy.

For our purpose, the practice of magic, it behooves us to connect as many aspects of this web into our spells as we can, those aspects that all jive at the same vibratory level. This includes the energy of the planets, days of the week, hours of the day, stones, herbs, colors, numbers, scents, etc. These connections are referred to as 'correspondences'; and the more correspondences that you include in your spell crafting, the more successful your spells will be.

It's all about energy and its movement...this is the secret of magic.

Magical Timing

Days of the Week/Hours of the Day

We'll begin with the hours after sunrise, the first chart. To find out what the hour of sunrise is in your area, check your local paper, weather station or the internet. Using that information, along with this chart, you'll know which planet's energy and influence is the strongest at any given hour of the day. Likewise, on the chart below this one, you'll find the hours after sunset. Check for the exact time the sun sets in your area and use the information from these charts to calculate the timing of your spell casting.

Hours after Sunrise

Sun.	Mon.	Tues.	Wed.	Thurs.	Fri.	Sat.
Sun	Moon	Mars	Mercury	Jupiter	Venus	Saturn
Venus	Saturn	Sun	Moon	Mars	Mercury	Jupiter
Mercury	Jupiter	Venus	Saturn	Sun	Moon	Mars
Moon	Mars	Mercury	Jupiter	Venus	Saturn	Sun
Saturn	Sun	Moon	Mars	Mercury	Jupiter	Venus
Jupiter	Venus	Saturn	Sun	Moon	Mars	Mercury
Mars	Mercury	Jupiter	Venus	Saturn	Sun	Moon
Sun	Moon	Mars	Mercury	Jupiter	Venus	Saturn
Venus	Saturn	Sun	Moon	Mars	Mercury	Jupiter
Mercury	Jupiter	Venus	Saturn	Sun	Moon	Mars
Moon	Mars	Mercury	Jupiter	Venus	Saturn	Sun
Saturn	Sun	Moon	Mars	Mercury	Jupiter	Venus

Hours after Sunset

Sun.	Mon.	Tues.	Wed.	Thurs.	Fri.	Sat.
Jupiter	Venus	Saturn	Sun	Moon	Mars	Mercury
Mars	Mercury	Jupiter	Venus	Saturn	Sun	Moon
Sun	Moon	Mars	Mercury	Jupiter	Venus	Saturn
Venus	Saturn	Sun	Moon	Mars	Mercury	Jupiter
Mercury	Jupiter	Venus	Saturn	Sun	Moon	Mars
Moon	Mars	Mercury	Jupiter	Venus	Saturn	Sun
Saturn	Sun	Moon	Mars	Mercury	Jupiter	Venus
Jupiter	Venus	Saturn	Sun	Moon	Mars	Mercury
Mars	Mercury	Jupiter	Venus	Saturn	Sun	Moon
Sun	Moon	Mars	Mercury	Jupiter	Venus	Saturn
Venus	Saturn	Sun	Moon	Mars	Mercury	Jupiter
Mercury	Jupiter	Venus	Saturn	Sun	Moon	Mars

Magical Ways for Magical Days

Although the roster of planets all contribute to the collective energies of every day, each day is influenced strongly by the vibrations of a specific planet, making particular days desirable for specific types of magic. Each day of the week is also heavily influenced by an element, color, astrological sign or signs, as well as herbs and even stones. Use this information when constructing a spell to raise the correct energy and vibrations needed to manifest your magic from the etheric plane to our physical world.

Sunday

    Color: yellow, gold
    Element: Fire
    Planet: Sun
    Herbs: frankincense, lemon, St. John's Wort, sunflowers
    Stones: citrine, amber, tiger eye
    Astrological Sign: Leo

Energies: healing, spirituality, male issues, work/employment, power, strength

Monday
Color: blue, white
Element: water
Planet: Moon
Herbs: moonwort, willow, violets, moonflowers
Stones: moonstone
Astrological Sign: Cancer
Energies: emotions, psychism, dreams, clairvoyance, the Goddess, feminine issues

Tuesday
Color: red, orange
Element: Fire
Planet: Mars
Herbs: dragon's blood, patchouli
Stones: carnelian
Astrological Sign: Scorpio
Energies: aggression, marriage (this is kind of ironic, isn't it?), courage, dominance, power

Wednesday
Color: silver, shades of blue
Element: Air
Planet: Mercury
Herbs: slippery elm
Stones: clear quartz crystal, malachite
Astrological Sign: Gemini, Virgo
Energies: communication, writing, art, creativity, mental activities

Thursday

Color: purple, indigo
Element: Fire
Planet: Jupiter
Herbs: cinnamon, nutmeg, sage
Stones: aventurine, moss agate
Astrological Sign: Sagittarius, Pisces
Energies: expansion, money, legal issues

Friday

Color: pink, red
Element: Air, Water
Planet: Venus
Herbs: rose, cardamom, catnip
Stones: pink rose quartz, jade
Astrological Sign: Libra, Taurus
Energies: love, friendship, emotions, beauty, sex

Saturday

Color: black, gray
Element: Earth
Planet: Saturn
Herbs: cayenne pepper, sulfur, poppy seeds, myrrh
Stones: black onyx, apache tears, obsidian
Astrological Sign: Capricorn
Energies: retribution, banishment, protection

Numbers

Numbers contain energy. They do. Certain numbers brought to mind have always produced different feelings in individuals. Some people cringe at the number '13', thinking it unlucky, while others find it desirable and magical. You must have met someone at one time who had a 'lucky number', or perhaps you yourself have one.

We win riches and fame with numbers, as with a lottery ticket; and men have been called to war, their fates sealed with a number, as in the draft of previous years.

The use of numbers in magic is relevant and highly significant to the essence of the energy that you're trying to create and the success of your spell crafting. Numbers correspond to planets, letters, elements, energies, and influences. Use the chart below when crafting your spells:

1...One

Planet: Sun
Element: Fire
Letters: a, j, s
Energies: developing the self, the All, wholeness, unity, beginnings

2...Two

Planet: Moon
Element: Water
Letters: b, k, t
Energies: duality, balance, couples, partnerships

3...Three

Planet: Jupiter
Element: Fire
Letters: c, l, u
Energies: health, triple aspects, psychism

4...Four

Planet: Uranus
Element: Air
Letters: d, m, v
Energies: quarters, foundations, the elements

5...Five

Planet: Mercury

Element: Air

Letters: e, n, w

Energies: communication, fulfillment

6...Six

Planet: Venus

Element: Water

Letters: f, o, x

Energies: emotions, magnetism, gods/goddesses, cats

7...Seven

Planet: Neptune

Element: Water

Letters: g, p, y

Energies: intuition, psychism, the dark side, shadow

8...Eight

Planet: Saturn

Element: Earth

Letters: h, q, z

Energies: material aspects, travel, protection, discipline

9...Nine

Planet: Mars

Element: Fire

Letters: i, r

Energies: aggression, conflict, dominance

Moon Magic

Once more my eighth-grade teacher, Sister Loretta, could never have foreseen how I would be putting to use the science lessons she gave about the moon almost forty years ago. But it all comes into play in the magical world, the world of the witch.

We all recognize the small celestial body that orbits the earth, bathing us in a wash of silver light in its full phase, and disappearing altogether on its dark night. The moon is approximately 221,000 miles from the earth at the nearest point in its orbit and nearly 252,000 miles from the earth at the farthest point.

The energy of the moon and its phases all influence the witch in the practice of her craft, what type of spells she casts and when, whether she's working with projective or receptive energy, even what aspect of the Goddess is highlighted and celebrated. We're going to look at the moon now with new eyes, with the eyes of a witch.

Moon Phases

Our mundane physical world, the earth, feels the waxing and waning energy of the moon, as expressed by the tides, by a woman's menstrual cycle – which mirrors the moon's phases – as well as by less-defined effects. Ask any police officer or emergency room nurse, and they will both assure you that they can tell when the moon is full by all the extra activity and incidents that occur on that night. This abundance of energy is also used by magical practitioners when casting spells, when determining the time to banish or the time to promote production. It's all about the moon's phases and timing magical spell casting to this rhythm.

The moon has eight phases, which are determined by the position of the moon in accordance with the earth and the sun. These phases include:

Full Moon
Waning Gibbous
Last Quarter
New Moon
Waxing Crescent

First Quarter
Waxing Gibbous

Each of these phases represents a waxing or waning of the moon's energy, a receptive or projective movement of will, shadow and light; the Goddess in her three faces; as well as the natural ebb and flow of a woman's body.

The Waxing Moon

Begins the day after the dark moon and culminates at the full moon.

This is a time of growth, when the moon is re-emerging from her dark phase, growing each evening in intensity and light. This is the time to do spells of invocation, of reception, a time to work magic to draw something *to* you.

The Waning Moon

Begins the day after the full moon and culminates on the new moon.

This is the time of release, when the moon is gradually pulling away, disappearing from the light. This is the time to do spells of banishment, of projection, a time to work magic to send something *away* from you.

Full Moon

The night of the full moon represents a culmination of the spells that were cast during the waxing phase. This is the time when the moon's energy is the most powerful, and if you have a will to match it, any magic you cast now will be especially strong, the energy volatile and quick. Witches celebrate the full moon with rituals called 'esbats'; and the night of the full moon is excellent for invocations…call that which you seek and it will come.

New Moon

The night of the dark moon represents a time to cast spells that will reveal secrets, a time to cast spells that will perpetuate beginnings. The time of the dark moon is also excellent for divination. Although some witches view this phase of the moon as a time to refrain from magic, the gray witch knows that now is the time to step into the shadows and grab the powerful energy found there.

Waning/Waxing Gibbous

These phases of the moon represent midway points, and these phases are often neglected by occult practitioners. In fact, the gibbous moons are times of great power, the waxing gibbous churning with building energy to be released at the full moon, and the waning gibbous receding, ready to release its energy on the night of the new moon. The gray witch takes advantage of these midway points, setting the stage for reception or projection, for manifestation or banishment.

The Moon Divine: The Triple Goddess

The energy of the moon has long been connected to the power of the feminine divine – the Goddess – in all her celestial glory and ancient ambiance. The moon's energy and phases coincide with the feminine at a physical, emotional, and psychic level that transcends time and has survived thousands of years of patriarchal spiritual dominance. Not only has the Goddess survived, but today she thrives, and a new generation is discovering the unique magic of her spirituality and, through that, their own connection to the moon and its energy.

There are three phases to the Goddess that coincide with the phases of a woman's life and to the moon's phases as well.

The Maiden

The Maiden is overflowing with all of the possibilities of the future. Within her are the seeds of what will be. She is the fresh dawn of a new day. She is strength and tenacity and power. She is unbridled enthu-siasm and wonder and hope.

The waxing crescent moon represents the Goddess in her aspect of Maiden and the beginning stage of a woman's life. This is her period of discovery, growth, and wonder. The world is just opening up before her, and she is about to start off, down her path, to discover her life and herself along the way.

The Mother

The Mother is ripe fruit hanging pregnant from the vine. She is the foundation, the nurturer, the protectress. She is fortified with strength and placid with the calmness of a sunny day. She is who we turn to for stability and reassurance.

The full moon, in all its glory, represents the Goddess as Mother; mature and fertile. She has come through the phase of Maiden and along the way has discovered her own strengths and her potential. During this phase of a woman's life she will take the role of creatrix, whether that which she creates is children, ideas, or projects.

The Crone

It is the Crone we seek in the darkening twilight. We find comfort in her quiet presence and yet we are challenged by her intuitive knowledge and aware of the dark shadows she casts – forcing us to seek the light and answers.

The waning crescent represents the Crone, and although some may view this phase as an ending, it is nothing of the kind. It is a culmination. At this phase of a woman's life she can relish and revel in her accomplishments. And even more importantly, she can pass on to the next generation the wisdom she has collected on her magnificent journey.

A Moon for Every Month

The energies and correspondences for the full moon of each month align with the passing of seasons and holidays, with astrology, numerology, the elements, and ancient traditions. Certain energies are highlighted and magnified with the full moon of each month. The time is ripe for spells of a specific nature and magical bent with the unfolding of each full moon. Use the following information when crafting spells, timing magic, or creating esbat rituals to celebrate the full moon.

January

Wolf Moon

Herbs: patchouli, lavender, pine, mimosa, peppermint

Stones: amethyst spirit quartz, garnet, cavansite, chrysanthemum quartz

Scents: musk, mimosa

Colors: white, indigo, black

Trees: birch

Deities: Freya, Inanna, Sarasvati, Hera, Ch'ang-O

Astrological Signs: Capricorn, Aquarius

Elements: Earth/Air

Crafting Your Magic:

The individualist will be highlighted with magic that's aimed at amplifying and celebrating nonconformity, originality, and creativity. This is an excellent time to work magic that will manifest clearer communication, magic that will promote better understanding between individuals, and magic that will heal rifts. Basic human needs can be emphasized with the Wolf Moon and now is the time for spells to ensure those needs are met through magical manifestation.

Work on issues this month that deal with the root chakra. The earthier side of sexuality is highlighted, as well as basic physical needs. Get down and dirty, familiarize yourself with the raw instinct of your basic nature.

February
Chaste Moon
Herbs: honeysuckle, oak moss, jasmine, nutmeg, pine
Stones: nebula stone, amethyst, ammolite, angelite
Scents: wisteria, heliotrope
Colors: light blue, violet
Trees: rowan, laurel, cedar
Deities: Brigit, Juno, Kuan Yin, Diana, Persephone, Demeter
Astrological Signs: Aquarius, Pisces
Elements: Air/Water

Crafting Your Magic:
Now's the time for spells to balance raw individualism with the dreamy and poetic side of life. Cast spells for divination, ambition, unrealized aspirations, and situations that will balance communication with emotion. Spells to reveal the truth and for clarity of vision may also be highlighted at this time. Magic aimed at the spiritual side of life will prove very strong with this moon. Now is the time to seek enlightenment and make some incredible magical connections with the Divine.

Work on issues this month that deal with the crown chakra, with illumination and enlightenment. Allow yourself to experience a sense of completion within the illusive energy of the spiritual side of life.

March
Seed Moon
Herbs: jasmine, star anise, sage, calamus, catnip
Stones: amethyst, aquamarine, pink fluorite
Scents: honeysuckle, apple blossom
Colors: light green, red-violet
Trees: alder, dogwood

Deities: Isis, the Morrigan, Hecate, Astarte, Artemis
Astrological Signs: Pisces, Aries
Elements: Water/Fire

Crafting Your Magic:
Just as water and fire may not mix well, so too some personalities suffer from conflicts and unresolved issues. Now is your opportunity to work on spells of reconciliation and spells to temper anger. This is also the perfect time for magic to enhance aggressiveness where it's called for, to work with dark magic for protection or retribution – you'll know which energy is needed where, trust me. The Seed Moon is the perfect time to work on issues of control, either to crush it where it's bothersome, or to take advantage of it for your benefit. Now is also the time to instill passion in all pursuits and endeavors, giving a magical charge to any projects.

The throat chakra could use some attention in the month of March, opening up communication and freeing a voice, or binding the hurtful words of a destructive personality. If you have issues when it comes to freely expressing yourself, now's the time to open up.

April
Hare Moon
Herbs: allspice, frankincense, fennel, musk, pine
Stones: diamond, crystalline kyanite, emerald
Scents: pine, bay, patchouli
Colors: red, gold
Trees: pine, bay, hazel
Deities: Kali, Hathor, Ceres, Venus, Bast
Astrological Signs: Aries, Taurus
Elements: Fire/Earth

Crafting Your Magic:

Magic during this time is all about transforming the energy of passion and will into physical manifestation. Anything you aspire to or desire will be brought into realization now through the passion of your emotions and the heat of your will – just be careful what you wish for. This is also the perfect time to cast a spell to banish stubbornness, either in yourself or someone you deal with. And at the other end of the spectrum, you can work magic now to instill a backbone where one might be lacking.

All seven chakras are highlighted during April. Work on those that show a blockage or need strengthening, or those chakras that you've had personal issues with in the past.

May

Fairy Moon
Herbs: apple blossom, magnolia, rose, vanilla, thyme
Stones: chrysolite, emerald, septarian
Scents: rose, sandalwood
Colors: green, brown, pink
Trees: hawthorn, apple
Deities: Bast, Venus, Aphrodite, Diana, Pan, Horned God, Artemis
Astrological Signs: Taurus/Gemini
Elements: Earth/Air

Crafting Your Magic:

The Fairy Moon magnifies duality. In this moon is the potential for personal growth, for illumination and wisdom. But the darker side of this energy is neurotic and complicated – handle with care. Cast magic now to unite logic and emotions, magic to emphasize the self and to banish bad habits, to strengthen self-esteem, and to reach personal goals. Work on magic that clarifies communication and highlights the solidity of reality with personal aspirations. This is also an excellent time for sex magic

– the energy of the God and Goddess is entwined, raw, and potent at this time.

The heart chakra is the energy center to concentrate on now. This chakra emphasizes relationships, love and friendship – and how you relate to both.

June

Mead Moon
Herbs: almond, dill, lily, lemongrass, clover
Stones: citrine herkimer, alexandrite, blue-lace agate
Scents: lily of the valley, lavender
Colors: orange, yellow-green
Trees: oak
Deities: Isis, Green Man, Cerridwen
Astrological Signs: Gemini, Cancer
Elements: Air/Water

Crafting Your Magic:

Fairy magic will be powerful and their presence could herald both the mystical and the mischievous. Work on magic now that clarifies communication and highlights the element of Air. Use magic of the wee folk to tap into the fairy realms. Magic now is all about movement – movement of ideas, creations, people, and places. This is the perfect time to cast spells of transformation, spells to increase/decrease, to banish/manifest. Think about where it is you want to be, either from a mental or physical perspective, and cast the magic needed to move you along to this destination.

The solar plexus is the chakras to focus on. Learn to assert yourself, or to tone down an overbearing attitude. And which energy applies to you? If you don't know, I'll bet the people around you do.

July

Herb Moon
Herbs: gardenia, myrrh, sandalwood, calamus, lemon balm
Stones: green calcite, ruby, peacock ore
Scents: orris, frankincense
Colors: silver, blue-gray
Trees: oak, acacia, ash
Deities: Cerridwen, Venus, Juno, Hel, Athene
Astrological Signs: Cancer/Leo
Elements: Water/Fire

Crafting Your Magic:

Balance ego with perseverance and organization in your spell work at this time. Manifest the power of leadership and banish indecisiveness. Now is when you will find empowerment from the strength of your emotions combined with a strong will and Leo's natural energy that leads to a desire for dominance.

Cast spells for long-term goals that will come to fruition at the Winter Solstice, manifesting with the return of the sun. Green witchcraft is highlighted with the Herb Moon. Revel in this magic. Tend to your herb gardens and flowerpots with tender loving care. Pluck and snip and dry, hanging bundles from the kitchen ceiling and stashing away in bottles and jars the ingredients for future spells and magical workings. The witch gathers to her now the botanicals that she will use during the course of the coming months and the inevitable winter.

August

Barley Moon
Herbs: rosemary, jasmine, lilac, violet, calamus
Stones: bronzite, peridot, green sapphire
Scents: frankincense, heliotrope
Colors: yellow, gold, green
Trees: hazel, alder, cedar

Deities: Ganesha, Hathor, Hecate, Nemesis
Astrological Signs: Leo, Virgo
Elements: Earth/Air

Crafting Your Magic:

The Barley Moon is the time to reap the harvest of magic cast at the beginning of the summer season. It's a time for the powerful assertive energy of Leo to give way to the calmer vibrations of Virgo. Do magic at this time to cleanse before the winter, cleansing not only your personal space, but intangible aspects as well. Clear out unwanted rubbish, whether it be inertia, conflict, indecisiveness, or some other personal weakness. As the summer winds down and wildlife begins to prepare itself for the dark months to come, this is where the heart of your magic lies as well.

September

Wine Moon
Herbs: lilac, mugwort, marjoram, rose, thyme
Stones: sapphire, bloodstone, rainbow obsidian
Scents: gardenia, rose, lilac
Colors: brown, yellow-green, amber
Trees: hazel, larch, bay
Deities: Demeter, Ceres, Isis
Astrological Signs: Virgo, Libra
Elements: Earth/Air

Crafting Your Magic:

Feminine energy is highlighted, receptive energy. Cast magic to draw inward, magic to draw to you those things – both intangible and material – that you need to fill the void. The Goddess is in the spotlight. Work magic to benefit female issues, such as fertility, independence, and protection.

The Wine Moon works its magic in the area of love and relationships. Cast spells to discover your soul mate, find a lost love, or nurture a secret desire. The energy of Libra will bring balance to all magic cast at this time, and its energy promotes the very essence of love and sex. Cast spells now to promote healthy sexuality and to maintain or regain physical health of the reproductive system.

Concentrate on the third-eye chakra, opening the doors to psychic experiences. Prepare to enter the autumnal dark months with the clairvoyant vision to see well beyond, into the light of the future.

October

Blood Moon

Herbs: ginger, myrrh, allspice, basil, clove

Stones: alexandrite, citrine, lilac kunzite

Scents: pine, patchouli

Colors: dark green, brown, gold

Trees: yew, cypress, maple, oak

Deities: Astarte, Horned God, Lakshmi, Ishtar

Astrological Signs: Libra, Scorpio

Elements: Air/Water

Crafting Your Magic:

Ancestral magic is cast with the Blood Moon. Do magic now to communicate with family members who have passed, to connect with your ancestors and your heritage. Magic surrounding divination is relevant; it's the perfect time. Cast spells for justice and balance, and to overthrow anything oppressive which may be blocking your path to success. Ambition is highlighted; use magic to increase the potency of your own, or cast magic to contain ambition that may have run amok. This is also the perfect time to step into the dark shadows and take advantage of the vibrations found there. The gray witch revels in the magic of the Blood Moon and in this season.

November

Snow Moon

Herbs: cumin, gardenia, vanilla, anise, sage

Stones: brown zircon, topaz, silver sheen obsidian

Scents: cedar, peppermint, hyacinth

Colors: gray, sage green

Trees: alder, cypress

Deities: Kali, Isis, Bast, Osiris, Sarasvati, Hecate

Astrological Signs: Scorpio, Sagittarius

Elements: Water/Fire

Crafting Your Magic:

Free yourself of those things that bind you, bind those things you need freedom from. Cast spells for release, relief, and emancipation; but make sure that you are not unintentionally restricting someone else's freedoms with your magic, your expectations, or your emotions – such as jealousy. Remember, your thoughts are pure energy and can set magical vibrations into motion.

Opposite energies are flying high during the Snow Moon. Use the vibrations generated from this energy to your advantage – remember that 'opposites attract'. Protection magic cast during this time is especially effective and potent.

December

Oak Moon

Herbs: cedar wood, juniper, sage, star anise, carnation

Stones: lapis, smoky quartz, lazulite

Scents: violet, patchouli, frankincense, myrrh, rose geranium

Colors: red, white, black

Trees: pine, fir, holly

Deities: Hathor, Hecate, Athene

Astrological Signs: Sagittarius, Capricorn

Elements: Fire/Water

Crafting Your Magic:

Balance carefully the energy of the traditionalist and that of the free spirit. Cast magic to seek knowledge from your ancestors, or to contact your spirit guide; cast magic to temper loyalties, and to reveal true feelings. Use magic now to throw light on shady situations and to call upon the energy of male divinity – the God. Magic for transitions is potent during the time of the Oak Moon. Work on long-term projects; now is the time to put into motion spells that will come into fruition with the Spring Equinox.

Note: The astrological signs listed with the moon months above are the zodiac sun signs ascribed to these time periods, and these are the basic energies that I work with. If you need to be more precise with the energy in your spell work or rituals, you should know that the moon moves through a new zodiac sign about every two and a half days, moving through all twelve signs in her 28.5-day cycle.

Consult an up-to-date almanac to know exactly what sign the moon is in at any given time…then take that energy and run with it.

What Is the Blue Moon?

As the moon moves through her cycle, which stays at a pretty steadfast 28.5 days, she is not always in sync with our calendar. The result of this is that one month out of every year we will have two full moons. The second full moon is called the blue moon.

'Once in a blue moon', as the old saying goes, means something which only happens once in a while, a rare occasion, something special. And that's exactly how the witch views the blue moon and the unexpected energy offered by its appearance.

Cast spells at this time to manifest once-in-a-lifetime opportunities, to reveal the dark side, ulterior motives, true friends, spirit contact, and to heighten divination. I modify correspondences used for spell crafting on the blue moon to the type of magic I'm creating and my intentions. There is a variety of magic to be cast upon this night. Listen to that little voice in your head; it knows something you don't.

Herbal Correspondences

Magic of the Green Witch

This is the magical medicine cabinet of the witch, and especially the Green Witch. Those who practice the 'Old Ways' have known since time immemorial of the powers contained in the molecules of 'the green'. Herbs have been used since ancient times, and are still used today, for their medicinal healing powers. But the witch knows that these gentle and lovely plants contain other powers as well – magical powers to be used and tapped into for spells and potions, rituals and cleansing.

The witch has a variety of ways that she incorporates the use of herbs in her practice, depending on her intentions and the plants used. Note that you should never ingest any herb, feed it to someone else, or even handle it with your bare hands, if you are not 100% sure that it is safe. Many herbs are edible, but there are just as many that are poisonous to ingest, and still others that can actually be absorbed through your skin, so handle with care. I abide by the old rule: 'When in doubt...don't.'

Once you've decided what type of spell you're going to cast, and you know exactly what your intentions are, then you'll have to decide which herbs will help you with this magic and how you're going to use them to your advantage.

How Do You Use the Herbs?

Charms and Sachets: Herbs are added to mojo bags or tied up in small cloth bundles for numerous intentions and carried in a purse, stuffed in a pocket, tucked beneath a pillow, hidden in the attic, laid upon your altar, or kept in a special place connected to your intentions. The use of herbs in the practice of magic is only limited by your own imagination and ingenuity.

Hanging in my vehicle is a mojo bag for safe travel containing calamus root and plantain, among other things. A bag for a good night's sleep might contain chamomile and valerian, and to induce dreams you may want to add a pinch of marigold blossoms; for a bag to draw love – catnip, cardamom, rose petals; for protection – rosemary; for prosperity – mint, poppy seeds, dill…and so it goes.

Incense: Herbs are ground and blended in numerous combinations to create an aromatic incense for rituals, specific intentions, or pure enjoyment. Witchcraft smells good – usually; this was one of my first impressions. But then you might find yourself creating concoctions that don't smell so good, or are 'unusual' to say the least, and these concoctions will do their work, dance their dance, and you'll love them just the same.

With homemade handmade incense, you might find that it works best when you blend this with a base, such as gum arabic, to hold the herbs together and make it easier to use; but you can do what I usually do, which is to simply sprinkle the blended dried herbs over the hot charcoal. You will want a mortar and pestle to grind and mix your herbs. Over the years, I've acquired several – one I use with poisonous herbs only, one with edible herbs, one for dark magic uses, and so on. I find mortars and pestles beautiful, from the one gifted to me by my mother and made of banded green onyx, to the white porcelain one that I use most often. You will also need a small fireproof container in which you can light a small disk of charcoal that you will burn this incense on. Don't confuse this charcoal and the regular old charcoal that you burn in your grill – they are two different things, and the charcoal for your grill is NOT safe to burn in an enclosed area. You can find the small charcoal disks you'll need at most new-age shops.

Baths and Washes: Herbs are dropped into bathwater in tea balls or bundles, or sprinkled liberally directly into your water for healings, cleansings, and numerous other intentions. I must warn you here that you should be knowledgeable about the herbs you are using; don't use anything that would be irritating to your skin. For instance, 'hot' herbs – like cayenne pepper, or stinging herbs – like nettles, would not add to a pleasant bathing experience. If you run across anything that you are personally sensitive to, I'm betting you'll remember what it is and you won't use it again.

For cleansing I like rosemary, and I usually add a large freshly picked bundle from my own garden right to my bathwater; to heighten your psychic senses – lavender and marigold; to add the illusion of youth – catnip; to prepare you for a restful night's sleep – chamomile, etc.

You can also add herbs to the water that you use to scrub your floors and surroundings with: a little sage to your mop water will cleanse your floor of more than just dirt; it will clear your living space of negative energy. If there has been discord in your home, add a little valerian to promote a peaceful atmosphere; if you feel you need protection, throw a dash of salt and rosemary in your mop water.

My favorite use of herbs is to use them in the creation of magical oils. The base you use for your oils may depend on your intentions – when making Black Cat Oil for protection, use castor oil; if you're making it to draw romance into your life, use almond oil. Grape seed oil makes another wonderful base, though it's a bit expensive. If you're pinched for funds, you can use olive oil, or even a cheaper oil from the grocery store.

Sometimes I've felt the need to heat the oil in my cast-iron cauldron on the stovetop and add the herbs to it, heating it just enough to release their energy and their scent. Other times I've simply filled a jar with oil, the appropriate herbs and occasional objects, and left the jar to sit in the sunlight – or the moonlight –

to charge it.

Either way…the magic works.

Teas: This is one of the most delightful ways to use herbs, by making a delicious old-fashioned pot of tea. And it's in this type of use that you must be very cautious about what herbs you're using. Make darn sure that you are 100% positive that the herbs you're adding to your pot of tea are edible and harmless.

Along with concocting my own homemade teas, I've bought many prepared teas from the grocery store or health food shop with magical intentions in mind. To these prepared teas you can add an extra herb or two, a pinch of this, a pinch of that; work your will and magical intentions into the ingredients: to call up prophetic dreams, throw a marigold blossom into your cup of tea before bedtime; to tame the wanderlust in your partner's eyes, give them a cup of tea laced with nutmeg or raspberries to insure fidelity; to dispel negative energy picked up from a hectic day, add fennel to your tea – you get the idea.

On Sundays my husband makes the morning coffee, and he usually steps out into our herb garden to snatch a handful of mint leaves that he adds to the basket of coffee grounds. This might sound strange, but after he uses a spoonful of hot coco as the creamer, it is the most delicious cup of coffee you'll ever have – and along with the mint comes energy for prosperity, wealth, and blessings.

Smoking: Shamans and spiritualists have smoked herbs for millennia for the purpose of vision questing, altering the subconscious mind, and opening themselves up to enlightenment. I have friends, dear witches – mothers, grandmothers, crones – who burn such herbs as mugwort before rituals or during divination sessions to benefit from the magic of the smoke. Native Americans may still legally use peyote, a very potent hallucinogen, during their spiritual rituals and vision quests.

Quite frankly, this is as far as I can go on this particular use of herbs. I've never smoked anything, not even a cigarette, in my fifty-three years. I warn against ingesting/smoking illegal or dangerous herbs for any reason. As with all things in life – use some common sense.

The Herbs

The following herbs are taken straight from the list in my own Book of Shadows. I have personally used all of the herbs listed here at some time or other, in some way or other, during my spell crafting and magic making. Aside from the standard correspondences, I've uncovered subtle nuances of the energies involved with these herbs. I've experienced unusual or unexpected results, as well as previously unlisted uses for some of the very common herbs. I accidentally stumbled upon this knowledge in the midst of my boiling cauldron and bubbling potions. When you begin crafting herbal magic, I'm sure this will be your experience as well. It's all part of working with the magic of 'the green'.

Allspice
(*Pimenta officinalis* or *P. fioica*)
Energy: projective/masculine
Planet: Mars
Element: Fire
Powers: money, luck, healing, relieves mental stress

Anise
(*Pimpinella anisum*)
Energy: projective/masculine
Planet: Jupiter
Element: Air
Power: protection, purification, youth, the Crone, spirit contact, deflects negative energy, psychism

Basil

(*Ocimum basilicum*)
Energy: projective/masculine
Planet: Mars
Element: Fire
Power: love, exorcism, wealth, protection, fidelity, family
   magic

Bay

(*Lauris nobilis*)
Energy: projective/masculine
Planet: Sun
Element: Fire
Power: protection, psychic powers, healing, purification,
   strength, Yule, Imbolc, induces visions, marriage

Cardamom

(*Elettaria cardamomum*)
Energy: receptive/feminine
Planet: Venus
Element: Water
Power: lust, love, beauty

Catnip

(*Nepeta cataria*)
Energy: receptive/feminine
Planet: Venus
Element: Water
Power: cat magic, love, beauty (youth), happiness

Cinnamon

(*Cinnamomum zeylanicum*)
Energy: projective/masculine
Planet: Sun

Element: Fire

Power: spirituality, success, healing, power, psychic powers, lust, protection, love

Clover

(*Trefoil*)

Energy: projective/masculine

Planet: Mercury

Element: Air

Power: protection, love, fidelity, exorcism, success; red clover: love and marriage; white clover: protection from evil and crossed conditions

Cloves

(*Eugenia caryophyllus*)

Energy: projective/masculine

Planet: Jupiter

Element: Fire

Power: protection, exorcism, money, love (fidelity), banishing/ releasing

Coriander

(*Coriandrum sativum*)

Energy: projective/masculine

Planet: Mars

Element: Fire

Power: love, health, healing, fidelity

Cumin

(*Cuminum cyminum*)

Energy: projective/masculine

Planet: Mars

Element: Fire

Power: protection, fidelity, exorcism, protection against theft

Dill

(*Anethum graveolens*)
Energy: projective/masculine
Planet: Mercury
Element: Fire
Power: protection (especially for children), money, lust, love, fertility, removing crossed conditions, legal issues, health

Fennel

(*Funicular vulgare*)
Energy: projective/masculine
Planet: Mercury
Element: Fire
Power: protection, healing, purification, wards off negativity

Frankincense

(*Boswellia carterii*)
Energy: projective/masculine
Planet: Sun
Element: Fire
Power: protection, exorcism, spirituality, anointing, Yule, visions, strength, wards off enemies or troublesome people in authority

Geranium

(*Pelargonium maculatum* or *P. odoratissimum*)
Energy: receptive/feminine
Planet: Venus
Element: Water
Power: fertility, health, love, protection

Ginger

(*Zingiber officinale*)
Energy: projective/masculine

Planet: Mars

Element: Fire

Power: love, money, success, power, psychic power, deflection, return-to-sender, spirit contact, quickens spell work

Ginseng

(*Panax quinquefolius*)

Energy: projective/masculine

Planet: Sun

Element: Fire

Power: love, wishes, healing, beauty, protection, lust, accentuates sexual charms

Lavender

(*Lavandula officinalis*)

Energy: projective/masculine

Planet: Mercury

Element: Air

Power: love, protection, sleep, chastity, longevity, purification, happiness, peace

Lemon Grass

(*Cymbopogon citratus*)

Energy: projective/masculine

Planet: Mercury

Element: Air

Power: repels snakes, lust, psychic power, brings good luck in love, clears crossed conditions

Licorice

(*Glycyrrhiza glabra*)

Energy: receptive/feminine

Planet: Venus

Element: Water

Power: lust, love, fidelity, grants control over a person or situation

Marigold

(*Calendula officinalis*)

Energy: projective/masculine

Planet: Sun

Element: Fire

Power: protection, prophetic dreams, legal matters, psychic power, Otherworld, fairy magic, Beltane

Mint

(*Mentha spp.*)

Energy: projective/masculine

Planet: Mercury

Element: Air

Power: money, prosperity, healing, travel, exorcism, protection, breaks jinxes

Mugwort

(*Artemisia vulgaris*)

Energy: receptive/feminine

Planet: Venus

Element: Earth

Power: psychic powers, protection, prophetic dreams, healing, astral projection, cleanses divination tools, spirit contact, divination, Litha, Dark Goddess

Myrrh

(*Commiphora myrrha*)

Energy: receptive/feminine

Planet: Moon

Element: Water

Power: protection, exorcism, healing, spirituality, Imbolc, Mabon

Nutmeg
(*Myristica fragrans*)
Energy: projective/masculine
Planet: Jupiter
Element: Fire
Power: luck, money, health, fidelity

Orange
(*Citrus sinesis*)
Energy: projective/masculine
Planet: Sun
Element: Fire
Power: love, divination, luck, money

Peony
(*Paeonia officinalis*)
Energy: projective/masculine
Planet: Sun
Element: Fire
Power: protection (use the root), exorcism, health, luck

Poppy
(*Papaver spp.*)
Energy: receptive/feminine
Planet: Moon
Element: Water
Power: fertility, love, sleep, money, luck, invisibility, visions, causes confusion (the seeds)

Raspberry
(*Rubus idaeus* or *R. serious*)

Energy: receptive/feminine
Planet: Venus
Element: Water
Power: protection, love, menstrual issues, fidelity
Note: Raspberry tea should not be ingested by pregnant women, as it can bring on uterine contractions.

Rose

(*Rosa spp.*)
Energy: receptive/feminine
Planet: Venus
Element: Water
Power: love, psychic powers, luck, protection, sexual attraction

Rosemary

(*Rosmarinus officinalis*)
Energy: projective/masculine
Planet: Sun
Element: Fire
Power: protection, love, lust, mental powers, exorcism, purification, healing, sleep, youth, empowers women

Sage

(*Salvia officinalis*)
Energy: projective/masculine
Planet: Jupiter
Element: Air
Power: immortality, longevity, wisdom, protection, wishes, purification, exorcism, Mabon, empowers women, reverses spells

Slippery Elm

(*Ulmus fulva*)

Energy: receptive/feminine
Planet: Saturn
Element: Air
Power: halts gossip/slander/libel/lies, enhances eloquence

St. John's Wort
(*Hypericum perforatum*)
Energy: projective/masculine
Planet: Sun
Element: Fire
Power: health, protection, strength, love, divination, happiness

Thyme
(*Thymus vulgaris*)
Energy: receptive/feminine
Planet: Venus
Element: Water
Power: healing, psychic powers, purification, creates irresistibility to an object/person, wards off negativity, Litha, aids sleep

Valerian
(*Valeriana officinalis*)
Energy: receptive/feminine
Planet: Venus
Element: Water
Power: love, sleep, purification, protection, purging

Wormwood
(*Artemisia absinthium*)
Energy: projective/masculine
Planet: Mars
Element: Fire

Power: psychic powers, protection, love, calling spirits, binding, divination, Dark Moon, Samhain, spirit invocation

A Stone's Throw

Energies of the Earth

Just as herbs hold specific energies that can be used in the metaphysical practice of witchcraft to manifest magic, likewise, stones also hold this power.

Following you will find a list of stones from my own Book of Shadows. I've not only used the energies of these stones to craft spells; I also use the power of these stones on a daily basis, as talismans and amulets, by wearing them in rings, pendants, bracelets, as well as by carrying them in my pocket, or placing them about my home, car, and work area.

Introduce yourself to these stones and listen to what they have to tell you.

Amazonite

Energy: receptive/feminine
Planet: Uranus
Element: Earth
Chakra: solar plexus
Zodiac: Virgo
Power: gambling, success, female energy, fine-tuning mental processes, regulating metabolism

Amber

Energy: projective/masculine
Planet: Sun
Element: Fire/Akasha
Chakra: throat
Zodiac: Leo, Aquarius

Power: Luck, healing, strength, protection, beauty, strengthening/breaking spells

Amethyst

Energy: receptive/feminine
Planet: Jupiter
Element: Water
Chakra: third eye, crown
Zodiac: Aquarius, Pisces
Power: dreams, addictions, psychism, healing, spirituality, meditation, positive energy

Aventurine

Energy: projective/masculine
Planet: Mercury
Element: Air
Chakra: heart
Zodiac: Aries
Power: money, mental powers, healing, luck, tempers pride

Bloodstone

Energy: projective/masculine
Planet: Mars
Element: Fire
Chakra: heart, aligns lower chakras
Zodiac: Aries, Libra, Pisces
Power: legal matters, wealth, business, invisibility, blood/ heart health, balances the chakras, curbs obsessive behavior

Carnelian

Energy: projective/masculine
Planet: Sun
Element: Fire

Chakra: sacral

Zodiac: Taurus, Cancer, Libra, Scorpio

Power: sexual energy, healing, protection, eloquence, controlling the mind

Chalcedony

Energy: receptive/feminine

Planet: Moon

Element: Water

Chakra: cleanses and aligns all chakras

Zodiac: Cancer, Sagittarius

Power: travel, protection, nightmares, spiritual/artistic creativity

Citrine

Energy: projective/masculine

Planet: Sun

Element: Fire

Chakra: cleanses and aligns all chakras

Zodiac: Aries, Gemini, Leo, Libra

Power: psychism, protection, nightmares, induces dreams, improves creativity

Crystal Quartz

Energy: projective/masculine, receptive/feminine

Planet: Sun, Moon

Element: Fire, Water

Chakra: aligns all chakras and the aura

Zodiac: all twelve sun signs

Power: protection, healing, power, psychism, vision quests, divination, cleanses auras, transmits energy

Garnet

Energy: projective/masculine

Planet: Mars
Element: Fire
Chakra: root
Zodiac: Aquarius
Power: healing, protection, strength, balances energy, dreams, love and bonding, self-esteem/self-confidence

Jade

Energy: receptive/feminine
Planet: Venus
Element: Water
Chakra: heart
Zodiac: Aries, Taurus, Gemini, Libra
Power: love, healing, longevity, wisdom, protection, prosperity, safe travel, astral travel, relieves stress

Kunzite

Energy: receptive/feminine
Planet: Venus
Element: Earth
Chakra: heart, aligns heart chakra with throat and third eye
Zodiac: Taurus, Leo, Scorpio
Power: relaxation, grounding, peace, meditation, past life, balances emotions, spirituality

Lapis Lazuli

Energy: receptive/feminine
Planet: Venus
Element: Water
Chakra: throat, third eye, crown
Zodiac: Sagittarius
Power: psychism, healing, fidelity, protection, power, aura cleansing

Malachite

Energy: receptive/feminine

Planet: Venus

Element: Earth

Chakra: heart

Zodiac: Scorpio, Capricorn

Power: business, success, power/protection, peace, vision quests, meditation, prosperity

Moonstone

Energy: receptive/feminine

Planet: Moon

Element: Water

Chakra: third eye

Zodiac: Cancer, Libra, Scorpio

Power: psychism, divination, love, moon magic, youth, beauty, wishes, the feminine, goddess magic

Onyx

Energy: projective/masculine

Planet: Mars

Element: Fire

Chakra: (none)

Zodiac: Leo

Power: defensive magic, self-control, protection, slowing the libido, justice, dreams/meditation, balancing energy

Rhodochrosite

Energy: projective/masculine

Planet: Mars

Element: Fire

Chakra: heart, clears solar plexus and root

Zodiac: Leo, Scorpio

Power: Love, peace, friendship, heart chakra, heals trauma,

balances male/female energy

Ruby

Energy: projective/masculine
Planet: Mars
Element: Fire
Chakra: heart, root
Zodiac: Aries, Aquarius, Leo, Cancer
Power: wealth, protection, love/lust, creativity, energy of
   passions (not just sexual passions), intuition, spiritual
   wisdom

Sapphire

Energy: receptive/feminine
Planet: Moon
Element: Water
Chakra: throat
Zodiac: Virgo, Libra, Sagittarius
Power: psychism, meditation, defensive magic, money, love,
   material manifestation

Selenite

Energy: receptive/feminine
Planet: Moon
Element: Water
Chakra: crown
Zodiac: Taurus
Power: energy, healing, reconciliation, meditation/visual-
   ization, reflects negativity, accents reality, dissolves guilt

Tiger Eye

Energy: projective/masculine
Planet: Sun
Element: Fire

Chakra: third eye

Zodiac: Leo, Capricorn

Power: legal issues, business, money, protection, luck, grounding, stability

Tourmaline

Tourmaline is found in a variety of colors, and each carries its own unique energy and has its own correspondences.

Energy: *pink* – receptive/feminine, *red* – projective/masculine, *green* – receptive/feminine, *blue* – receptive/feminine, *black* – receptive/feminine

Planet: *pink*/Venus, *red*/Mars, *green*/Venus, *blue*/Venus, *black*/Saturn

Element: *pink*/water, *red*/fire, *green*/earth, *blue*/water, *black*/earth

Chakra: protects all of the chakras

Zodiac: *pink*/Cancer; *red*/Aquarius; *green*/Leo, Cancer; *blue*/Libra

Power: *pink*/love and friendship, creativity, personal freedom; *red*/energy, courage, strengthens will, protective rituals, self-confidence, inspiration; *green*/money, success, business, creativity, deflects negative energy; *blue*/relaxation, rest, sleep, creativity, psychism, spirituality; *black*/protection, grounding, releasing negative energy, prosperity, deflects negative energy

Turquoise

Energy: receptive/feminine

Planet: Venus

Element: Earth

Chakra: throat, third eye

Zodiac: Scorpio, Sagittarius, Pisces

Power: healing, friendship, love, protection, communication

Zircon

Energy: projective/masculine
Planet: Sun
Element: Fire
Chakra: unites base, solar plexus, and heart
Zodiac: Sagittarius
Power: sexual energy, healing, beauty, love, protection, spiritual insight

A Special Crystal
Salt

Energy: receptive/feminine
Element: Earth
Power: purification, protection, grounding, prosperity

Salt is a mineral; it's a mineral with a crystal structure. Salt may be considered one of the most important items in a witch's magical cupboard.

The primary power of salt is purification. You will use a pinch of salt in a small bowl of water to asperge and cleanse the ground for your sacred space. Salt is used in baths to purify the witch for rituals; it's sprinkled about her living space to cleanse and keep away negative energy and entities.

Salt draws money and prosperity, and it's said that you should never run out of salt, for if you do you will also run out of money. I keep an unopened container of salt in the dark recesses of my kitchen cupboard. It's not to be used; it's only there to insure continued prosperity in my household.

A word of caution: Salt is very grounding. If you are psychic, you may notice that ingesting salt prior to giving a reading will impede your intuitive abilities. If you wish to strengthen and enhance your psychic powers, limit your intake of salt. Also, if you're deliberately invoking spirits, you should know that salt will keep them at bay.

We live in a house that has always manifested a lot of paranormal activity. Over the years, when any of my children have been bothered during the night by restless or mischievous spirits, I would sit a bowl of salt on the night table beside their beds. I told them that there's nothing to be afraid of: just throw a pinch of salt at the apparition and it will go away. Not only did my children learn how to clear their living space of unwanted entities; they also discovered personal power in the fact that they have control over their environment.

The Wheel of the Year
The holidays celebrated today by Christians have their roots firmly planted in Pagan tradition. This is a fact that was constantly brought up to me years ago by a lady who was my friend and a Jehovah's Witness. It was her oft-repeated reason why she didn't celebrate any of the modern Christianized holidays.

I'm surprised by the number of people who are not aware of this and even more surprised at how many people refuse to believe this information when it's revealed to them. It just goes to show how completely saturating cultural training can be. I find the history of our Pagan holidays joyful and inspirational. Below you will find the eight Sabbats (holidays) celebrated today in all their Pagan glory around the world.

Samhain
(pronounced Sou-wen)
October 31
Also known as: Halloween, All Hallow's Eve, The Celtic New Year, The Witches' New Year
Traditions: celebrating summer's end, honoring your ancestors, celebrating preparations for winter, honoring the Crone aspect of the Goddess, divination, transformation, and regeneration.

Pagan Lore:

Jack-o-lanterns...the early Pagans used gourds instead of pumpkins. Frightening faces were carved upon them to frighten away malevolent earthbound spirits.

Apples...it's believed that dunking for apples was a form of Pagan initiation called 'seining', similar to baptism. It's only right that the apple would have been used for this purpose. The apple is the fruit of the Goddess, and Samhain is a time to celebrate her aspect as Crone. Slice an apple in half across the middle, and you will reveal a pentagram – a five-pointed star, the Pagan symbol for the four elements and the Divine.

Black and orange...the traditional Halloween colors of today. But these colors also date back to the Pagans. Black represents death, magic, and the Crone; orange is the color of the harvest and the God.

Costumes...the Celtic New Year was seen as a time of new beginnings. It's believed that wearing a costume, transforming yourself, symbolized the fact that you could start over, begin anew, and become anything you put your mind to. It's also believed that by wearing costumes at Samhain, you could disguise yourself from malevolent spirits.

Trick-or-Treating...on this night the poor would go door to door, begging for food, and they would be given pastries and 'treats'. In return they promised to say prayers for the dead.

The witches' celebration of Samhain has a more somber side than the revelry of modern-day Halloween. This is a day of remembrance to honor your ancestors, as well as family members who have passed over. Pagan families may set an extra plate at the supper table on this evening in remembrance of a loved one, opening a place for the departed spirit to join them on this magical night. They may also create altars in their homes with old family photos and memorabilia to honor deceased relatives.

The veil between the world of the living and the dead is thinnest on Samhain night, and this is an excellent time to try to establish contact with the other side. Samhain is also an auspicious time for divination, for on this night the energy of psychics and clairvoyants is magnified, more open and free flowing.

Samhain night encompasses that which is normally not seen, and reveals secrets generally hidden in the mists of our mundane world. It is truly the most magical night of the year.

Winter Solstice

December 21 (approx.)

Also known as: Yule

Traditions: celebrating the return of the sun, burning the Yule log, casting blessings to insure bountiful crops and healthy livestock in the coming year

Pagan Lore:

The Yule log...this was burned to celebrate the rebirth of the Sun God, and to herald a return of warmth and light to the earth.

Evergreen trees...this tree represents longevity and eternal life. Evergreen trees were decorated with lit candles, fruits, nuts, and other ornaments to celebrate the return of the Sun God. This tree was often topped with a five-pointed star, the symbol of the four elements and Divinity.

Exchanging gifts...it's believed that this tradition began with the Feast of Saturnalia, a Roman celebration to honor the god Saturn, held around the time of the Winter Solstice. Candles were given as gifts, representing 'light', as well as figs, nuts, and coins.

Red, white, and green...red represents the Goddess in her aspect of Mother; red also generates energy, passion, lust, love, and strength of will. White represents the Goddess as Maiden and also symbolizes purification, protection, peace and longevity. Green brings the energy of health, healing, wealth and prosperity, as well as luck.

The day of the Winter Solstice is the longest night of darkness or the shortest day in the year; and with the darkness comes the promise of light, the rebirth of the Sun. It's no wonder, because of the importance of this date to the ancient Pagans and the symbolism involved, that the Roman Church chose this date to celebrate the birth of Christ. With the return of the sun, the end of the dark cold winter is in sight. In ancient times, winter was a much harsher reality that brought with it hunger and death. But with the coming of the solstice, hope and promise are born. It's a time of revelry and celebration.

The most famous Winter Solstice celebration is held at Stonehenge, where large crowds of people, who have come from all over the world, will await the sunrise.

The time of the Winter Solstice is related to the epic mythic battle between the Holly King – who rules the dark months; and his brother, the Oak King – who rules the months of light. They will wage their battle, and during the Winter Solstice it is the Oak King who will prevail, the victor, bringing light and warmth back into the world...and with it next spring's growing season.

Imbolc
February 2
Also known as: Candlemas
Traditions: candle rituals, celebrating the end of winter, performing purification rituals, and making offerings to the Divine

Pagan Lore:
The groundhog...in ancient times the woodchuck was used as a method of divination to determine what the remainder of winter weather would hold in store. When Pagans arrived in the new world, the groundhog was used as a substitute for this tradition.

Candles...candles are used in rituals to invoke the goddess Bride, or Saint Brighid. Traditionally the candles were held near the throat to prevent colds and other maladies.

Bonfires...Bride is honored by bonfires, fire being a symbol of purification and cleansing. It's thought that the custom of 'spring cleaning' derived from the fires of purification. Indoor work would be done at this time so everyone would be able to devote the coming months to nurturing this year's food supply in their fields and gardens.

In the ancient world, and in the agricultural world of today, this is the time when the ewes begin giving birth. Not only is the miracle of birth the center of this Sabbat, but the accompanying wonder of lactation is celebrated as well. This is also a festival of the Celtic goddess Bride, so beloved by the people of the old world that the Roman Church couldn't eradicate her. Instead they made her a saint, Saint Brighid. In Celtic lore, the Old Woman of Winter (the Cailleach) was reborn as Bride, the Young Maiden of Spring.

Springtime is often representative of new beginnings, and for many Wiccan groups this is a popular time for initiations to take place.

Spring Equinox

March 21 (approx.)

Also known as: Eastre, Ostara

Traditions: coloring and decorating eggs, celebrating sunrise rituals, fertility rites, making offerings to the Goddess of Spring

Pagan Lore:

'Easter'...the Teutonic Goddess of Spring is known as Eastre, Eostre, and in some traditions, Ostara.

Fasting...with the return of spring and animals coming out of hibernation, people of the ancient world looked forward to eating fresh meat. They would fast before the Ostara celebrations to cleanse their systems and to put themselves in an altered state of consciousness to work magic at this time.

Rabbits and eggs...these two symbols of fertility need little explanation. However, the egg was not only a symbol of fertility but of transformation and resurrection as well.

At the Spring Equinox, the period of light and dark are equal and after this point light will begin to dominate the days ahead, heralding springtime planting and a promise of warmth returning with the summer months. This is a period of resurrections, when animals emerge from their winter sleep, when crops begin to sprout from the earth, and when fertility is celebrated with the birth of livestock.

Eggs will be dyed in many Pagan homes in celebration of Ostara; and they will be magically empowered for health and prosperity, as well as other blessings. Dawn rituals will be observed by some, along with garden/seed blessings, and bonfire rituals highlighting goals and aspirations for the year ahead.

In some traditions it's believed that now is the time the God and Goddess embrace and conceive the Sun God, who will be born at the Winter Solstice. It's also interesting to note why the date for the Christian holiday of Easter moves every year – Easter is always celebrated on the first Sunday after the first full moon after the Spring Equinox.

There's no escaping our Pagan roots.

Beltane

May 1

Also known as: May Day

Traditions: love/sex magic, leaping the bonfire to bring luck, dancing round the Maypole, honoring garden and house spirits, fertility magic

Pagan Lore:

The Maypole...in ancient Irish history there was a sacred tree believed to be the forerunner of the Maypole. It was thought that dancing around this tree on Beltane would send energy to the womb of the Earth and awaken her.

May Day baskets...comes from the ancient Beltane Eve tradition of a young man leaving a garland of flowers at the door of a young woman who has caught his eye. This was an invitation, and if accepted, the young couple would steal away for a night together in the forest, awaiting the Beltane sunrise. In modern times, the garland was replaced with a basket of sweets.

Youth and beauty...it's said that at sunrise on the morning of Beltane, those women wishing to recapture their youth, as well as all women wishing to retain their beauty, should go out into the grass at the break of dawn, sweep up the morning dew within their hands, and bathe their faces with it.

This holiday is one of the most Pagan. It is a celebration of fertility. To the modern world, it's more commonly known as May Day.

What the Roman Church tried so hard to control, to portray as evil, sinful, or dirty, is the very thing celebrated at Beltane: human sexuality. The ancient rites of Beltane celebrate the copulation of the God and the Goddess (the priest and the priestess); and in some Wiccan traditions this celebration of sexuality is honored with a ritual known as The Great Rite.

What was once considered wonderfully human, delightful, a miracle of life, and in some cases a spiritual act, was degraded by the Roman Church, the same church which branded women as evil and with it the emotions of lust and passion.

Modern-day Pagans have reclaimed the celebration of human sexuality and the miracle of fertility that accompanies it. People still dance around the Maypole, a phallic symbol, while they hold brightly colored streamers spilling from the top of this pole, symbolic of the creative force of sex.

Summer Solstice

June 21 (approx.)

Also known as: Midsummer's Eve

Traditions: Love magic, invocation/celebration of fairies and nature spirits, bonfires

Pagan Lore:

The Holly King and the Oak King...representing the waxing and waning energy of nature, are at it again. These brothers will battle once more, and this time it is the Holly King who will win, bringing with his victory gradually shortening days and eventually a return to the winter season.

This is the longest period of daylight in the year, a time of magic, fairies, and the immortalized Midsummer's Eve. Fairy contact is generally easier to achieve on this day, for those of you who wish to invoke the mischievous little folk, that is. But don't be surprised if soon after you can't find your favorite earrings, or the car keys, or any other shiny inviting objects you may have left lying around.

This is a popular month for weddings, though few in the Christianized world realize why. The Druids celebrated the Summer Solstice as the 'marriage between heaven and earth', and thus the popular belief that June is a 'lucky' month for marriage ceremonies. There will be a happy plethora of Pagan handfastings and weddings during June, all filled with the promise of bounty and fertility, mirrored by the burgeoning gardens and flowerbeds of this month.

The most popular Pagan gathering will be at Stonehenge. Just as large groups of people gathered there for the Winter Solstice to welcome back the light, so will they gather again, bonfires roaring through the night, to await the dawn and another new cycle. At our house, when my son was still a boy, I would light a candle, place it in my cauldron, and set it beneath the large apple tree in our backyard. With this candle I would burn marigold blossoms, in hopes of attracting fairies and nature spirits. My son would settle himself in a chair beneath the tree and near the candle, waiting patiently to sight fairies on this night. I have to say that on a couple of occasions he had some rather remarkable experiences.

Lughnasadh

(pronounced Loona-saw)

August 1

Also known as: Lammas

Traditions: celebration of first harvest/grain harvest, celebration of the Feast of Bread, weather magic, gathering bilberries as a symbol of abundance, games showcasing athletic ability

Pagan Lore:

Lugh...Lughnasadh celebrates the Irish god Lugh, a god of strength and athletic prowess. Tradition has it that Lugh's mother Tailtiu passed to the Summerland while working in the fields preparing for the planting season.

This is the first of the harvest festivals, and in the ancient world this was indeed a time of celebration. A successful harvest would mean survival in the harsh winter months to come. In the northern countries this was a celebration of the first harvest of wheat and grain, thus bread is featured in the celebration of Lughnasadh, also known as Lammas. Freshly baked loaves of aromatic bread are the main feature found upon Pagan altars for this holiday.

As modern-day Pagans celebrate the festival of Lughnasadh, they will build roaring bonfires, feed each other a mouthful of bread, and with wine they will toast each other: *'May you eat the bread of life.'*

Autumn Equinox

September 21 (approx.)

Also known as: Mabon

Traditions: celebration of the second harvest festival of the season, thanksgiving for plentiful harvest; in some cultures this is a corn festival, marking the beginning of the autumn season, the witches' Thanksgiving.

Pagan Lore:

Descent of the Goddess...in Sumerian myth she's known as Inanna; in Greek/Roman legends it was Demeter and Persephone. The descent of the Goddess into the Underworld meant an end to the lush growing season, a time when nature would rest beneath the cloak of winter.

The Harvest Lord...in the Celtic tradition, the Harvest Lord was slain at the time of Lughnasadh, marking the end of the growing season and the beginning of harvest time.

Mabon...is the masculine counterpart of Persephone; the fertile male aspect of the growing season. He is a Welsh god, stolen from his mother Modrin as an infant and, so the myth goes, rescued by King Arthur. All the while, he was held captive in the Otherworld – Modrin's womb – so as to be 'reborn' with the spring, bringing with him fertility to the land.

Wickerman...at this time of year, the ancient Druids would burn a large human-like wicker figure as part of their celebration. This figure represented the vegetation spirit, and indeed, the heralding of the dark season would bring an end to the growth and flowering of summer.

This day brings equal hours of light and dark, a second celebration of perfect equality. Beyond this day, light will gradually fade as the dark season descends upon the world. Modern Pagans celebrate this holiday with many of the foods connected with this time of year in their area. For us this would include pumpkin pie, pumpkin breads, and apple cider. Decorations may include leaves of autumn hues, sunflowers, pumpkins and gourds.

Part 2

Rituals

Rituals

We seek to find peace of mind in the word, the formula, the ritual.[2]

Rituals put a stamp on the passage of time and the progression of our life stages, from a wiccaning (a baby naming) to a death and remembrance ritual, and all those celebrations and milestones in-between. Rituals validate our existence in some implausible elusive way. They bring family and friends together, open doors to the future, reconnect us with the past, and create memories for generations to come.

For most of the following rituals you will find a list of special items needed for these occasions, in addition to your regular ritual tools.

Circle Casting

When a witch 'casts a circle', it means that she is setting boundaries and creating sacred space. She is cleansing and consecrating an area to be used for rituals, spell casting, or any other magical endeavor in which she desires protection, the assistance of Divinity in a very personal way, support from the Elementals and the four elements they represent, as well as the opportunity to access other planes of existence.

A magic circle holds the energy a witch raises until she is ready to release it. It keeps her safe from malevolent entities, which is particularly important for the gray witch when she is working with darker energies. Remember, only those entities that you invite may enter your circle. The Watchtowers at the four corners contribute their muscle, keeping your space free of unwanted presences and adding their energy to your spell crafting and rituals.

Within a magic circle you are 'outside of time'. When you stand in the midst of well-cast sacred space, you are literally standing 'between the worlds', between the etheric plane and the mundane world. Here you will be able to access the past, to move through worlds of various realities, to safely invoke gods and goddesses, as well as spirits. In the heart of the magic circle, the witch will come face to face with herself and the inherent power she possesses.

With that said, let's cast our circle...

Items needed:

1. Broom
2. Small bowl of water
3. Salt
4. Sprig of rosemary or sage
5. Athame or magic wand

1. Whether your circle is being cast in the middle of your living room, in a corner of your bedroom, or the laundry room downstairs, make sure that this space has been mundanely cleaned and tidied up, perhaps decorated for the occasion with appropriate flowers, herbs, magical décor, and of course, your working ritual tools.

If you are going to create your sacred space in the middle of a wild grove, an outdoor recreational area, or even your own backyard, you will want to make sure that you have enough privacy so as not to be disturbed.

2. Sweep the area with your besom (broom), whether this broom is a special ritual broom used only for this purpose, or – in hoodoo tradition – the mundane broom that you use every day. We're talking about energy here, sweeping away not the dirt on the ground or floor, but the negative energy lying about this space. I don't even touch the floor with my ritual broom, having done the mundane sweeping before I start. With my ritual broom, I sweep in long whooshing draughts from east to west, chanting while I sweep, moving negative energy out, out,

out...pushing it from this space. Order it out, claim this space, shove it, push it, bully it out. As I do this, I usually get a tingling rush from the soles of my feet up the calves of my legs. It amazes me every time.

3. Take a small bowl of water, add a pinch of salt to it, stirring it deosil (clockwise) with your finger. Now you're going to 'asperge' this area, that is you're going to sprinkle the water about this space to cleanse and consecrate it. You can either use your fingers, or you can use a sprig of rosemary or sage for this purpose.

4. Take your athame or magic wand and go to the elemental gateway of Earth. Stand in the center of this freshly cleansed area. Point your athame/wand to the north quarter, at the boundary of your circle, and begin. Slowly, moving deosil, make three passes around this area, following the boundary of your circle while chanting:
First pass:

'Earth, Air, Fire, Water, circle round
This blessed consecrated ground.'
Second pass:
'East, south, west, north;
Seal this space, bring power forth.'
Third pass:
'By the power of the witches' blade,
This ground is sealed, the circle made.'

Once your magic has been worked, your ritual complete, you must take the time to dismantle the sacred space that you've created. The energies here must be dispersed, sent back from whence they came, to be called forth at another time, another place.

Take your athame/wand in your power hand (your dominant hand). Stand in the center of the magic circle. Raising your arms aloft, point the blade at the north quarter, and with one sweeping gesture, following the boundary of your space, cut the energy of this circle widdershins (counter-clockwise) while saying:

> *'Disperse all energies*
> *To their rightful place;*
> *With appreciation,*
> *Love, and grace.*
> *Open now this sacred space.'*

Calling the Quarters

After casting your circle, you'll want to 'call the quarters', that is invoke the elementals and their energies at the four compass points of your sacred space. These are the Watchtowers, the protectors, the energies that add fuel to your magical workings and power to your rituals: Earth, Air, Fire, and Water.

Items needed:

1. Four candles: green, yellow, red, and blue
2. Athame or magic wand

North: Earth

Set a green candle at the north gate, the gate of Earth. Light this candle, raise your athame/wand or index finger in the air, and while drawing the invoking pentagram of Earth in the space above this candle say:

> *'Watchtowers of the North,*
> *I summon you now*
> *To this sacred place.*
> *Guard this circle*
> *Outside of time and space.*

By the powers of Earth,
To my magic give birth.'

East: Air

Set a yellow candle at the east gate, the gate of Air. Light this candle, raise your athame/wand or index finger in the air, and while drawing the invoking pentagram of Air in the space above this candle say:

'Watchtowers of the East,
I summon you now
To this sacred place.
Guard this circle
Outside of time and space.

By the powers of Air
Bring magic to bear.'

South: Fire

Set a red candle at the south gate, the gate of Fire. Light this candle, raise your athame/wand or index finger in the air, and while drawing the invoking pentagram of Fire in the space above this candle say:

'Watchtowers of the South,
I summon you now
To this sacred place.
Guard this circle
Outside of time and space.

By the powers of Fire,
My magic inspire.'

West: Water
Set a blue candle at the west gate, the gate of Water. Light this candle, raise your athame/wand or index finger in the air, and while drawing the invoking pentagram of Water in the space above this candle say:

'Watchtowers of the West,
I summon you now
To this sacred place.
Guard this circle
Outside of time and space.

By the powers of Water will be
Energy to set my magic free.'

Cakes and Wine
The idea of sharing a communion with deity by partaking of food and drink is an ancient custom and practice, not defined by, nor exclusive to, the Judeo-Christian religions of today. It's generally referred to as 'cakes and wine' or 'cakes and ale'. This ritual is viewed as a celebration of the union of the God – represented by the athame, and the Goddess – represented by the chalice.

A 'cakes and wine' ritual may be incorporated into any other ritual. It will highlight the celebration with a special connection to divinity.

Items needed:

1. Wine – or if preferred, a nonalcoholic beverage, such as grape juice
2. Bread/cookies/pastry, etc. If this is made especially for the ritual, you could add a pinch of an herb connected with a particular god/goddess, or an herb associated with the type of ritual you'll be celebrating when you have cakes

and wine.

3. A plate to hold the bread or pastry
4. Chalice
5. Athame

The basic ritual:

1. The Priestess stands at the altar and acknowledges the sacredness of the God and Goddess, saying:

'We gather here to draw strength and magic from the God...Father Sky, the power of the sun, who sends His energy out to us, that we may project magic and manifestation.

We gather here to draw strength and magic from the Goddess...Mother Earth, the power of the moon, who sends Her energy inward to us, that we may receive magic and manifestation.'

2. The Priestess will take up her athame, holding it high above the chalice of wine with both hands. While slowly lowering the tip of the blade into the chalice of wine, she will say:

'As the God finds joy and fulfillment in union with the Goddess, so shall the earth be fruitful and blessed.'

3. The Priestess shall then hold the athame in her hand, touching the tip of the blade to the bread, saying:

'As the Goddess finds joy and fulfillment in union with the God, so shall the earth be fruitful and blessed.'

4. All present shall share of the bread and wine, saving a small amount of each to pour out upon the earth as a libation.

Self-Initiation

Note: Read the entire initiation ritual through and become familiar with it before you perform it. Make sure you have gathered all of the required items – the oil, and candles, and such

– and that you feel prepared to step across the threshold of this mundane world.

Items needed:

1. Loose-fitting robe
2. Silver pendant, usually a pentacle
3. White pillar initiation candle
4. Witches' oil
5. Incense

The time has come, the day is here, to cement your devotion and commitment to the path of witch. You will have prepared the area of your sacred space for this ritual the day before, not only cleansing it mundanely, but ridding it of negative energy. You will decorate the altar and this space with those flowers, herbs, stones, statuary, and articles that ring with your vibrations and your personal inspirations.

The morning of your special day you will bathe with intent, cleansing not only your body, but your mind and your spirit as well; paving the way for purity of intent and application of personal power.

You will wear a long loose robe, one that can be easily shifted aside to expose those areas of the body to be anointed; or you will perform this ritual skyclad (naked). You will have purchased a silver pendant necklace as a symbol of your new position in life. This pendant may be a pentacle, or it may be a symbol that resonates more closely with your own energy.

When you have bathed and dressed yourself, and after you have taken some time to ground and center yourself, you will begin.

1. Cast your circle.

2. Call the quarters.

3. Light the tall white pillar candle upon your altar. This candle is representative of the Goddess, often called 'The Mother Candle'. Light your incense as well, representing the God. Your initiation pendant will lie upon the altar until you're ready for it.

4. Light the special candle that you've chosen as your initiation candle, saying:

'I, (name), have entered this circle in perfect love and perfect trust. I am ready to commit myself to the way of witch. I place myself now before the altar of the Goddess and the God, before the altar of the Ancient Ones, before the altar of the Powers that Be.'

5. Stand before the altar now and prepare to anoint yourself. Taking the bottle of oil from the altar, put some oil on your fingers and touch them to the tops of your feet, saying:

'Bless these feet,
created to walk the way of witch.'

Apply the oil to your knees, saying:

'Bless these knees,
created to kneel before the altar of the Goddess.'

Apply the oil to your genitals, saying:

'Bless this womb,
* the gateway to life.'*

(*Note:* If the initiate is a male, say:

'Bless this phallus,
Creator of life.')

Apply the oil to your breasts, saying:

'Bless these breasts and the heart beneath,
that my motives be pure
and my will be strong.'

Touch the oil to your forehead, tracing a pentagram upon it, and set the bottle of oil back upon your altar.

6. Take up your initiation pendant, holding it aloft, and stand

before the altar, saying:

'I, (name), do solemnly swear upon the blood of my ancestors to devote the rest of my days to living the way of witch.

I swear loyalty to the Ancient Ones, the gods and goddesses who always were, are now, and shall forever be.

I swear loyalty to my fellow witches: my sister-witches of the past, as well as those who touch my life today, and those I have yet to meet. I vow to keep their secrets, to learn from them as well as teach, to respect our differences, and to celebrate our journey together upon this sacred path.

I freely take upon myself the life of witch. As I turn the corner to live my destiny, I declare to the Powers present here that my magical name is (craft name).'

7. With your pendant in your hands, go now and stand before the gate of Earth. Raise your pendant aloft, saying:

'By the powers of Earth,
May I flourish in the physical realm.

'Guardians of the Gateway of Earth,
Know me,
I am (craft name)!'

Go now and stand before the gate of Air. Raise your pendant aloft, saying:

'By the powers of Air,
May I grow in knowledge and wisdom.

'Guardians of the Gateway of Air,
Know me,
I am (craft name)!'

Go now and stand before the gate of Fire. Raise your pendant aloft, saying:

'By the powers of Fire,
May I grow in passion and strength of will.

'*Guardians of the Gateway of Fire,*
Know me,
I am (craft name)!'
Go now and stand before the gate of Water. Raise your
pendant aloft, saying:
'*By the powers of Water,*
May I grow in intuition and second sight.

'*Guardians of the Gateway of Water,*
Know me,
I am (craft name)!'

8. Return now to the altar. Hold aloft your pendant, saying:
'*By Earth and Air, Fire and Water,*
Rejoice!
Upon this day, a witch is born –
(craft name)!
So Mote It Be.'

9. Put on your pendant necklace.

10. The ritual is finished. Take your time within the circle to
ground and center, to reflect, to absorb the experience. When you
are ready, dismiss the quarters, dismantle the circle. Go and eat
something to replenish your energy. And celebrate.

Drawing Down the Moon
The energy of the moon has long been connected with the radiant
energy and power of the Goddess. The witch – the priestess – has
developed methods to harness this energy, to draw this power
within herself and use it for personal growth and enlightenment.
    The following ritual will allow you to reconnect with the
Goddess and rediscover the magic and mystique of the feminine
divine.

1. To connect with moon energy, you must place yourself beneath its light, allowing your body to bathe within its silver sheen. As you do so, ground and center yourself.

2. Bless yourself, saying:
    'Bless my feet that walk the way of witch.
    Bless my knees that kneel before the Goddess.
    Bless my breasts that nurture
    and my lips that speak the truth.
    Before the Goddess,
    I am blessed.'

3. Stand with your feet slightly parted; raise your arms to the sky, hands open and receptive. Say:
    'I stand before You now, Mother of the Earth,
    To draw within myself the energy of rebirth.

    'The magic of the moon,
    The energy of goddess power,
    I draw down into myself,
    Upon this shining hour.'

4. Stand for a few minutes where you are. You may feel physical sensations that are unique to this ritual and goddess energy, or you may feel sensations that are common during the movement of energy and the acquisition of power. Don't be disappointed, however, if you have no physical sensations at all; not everyone is sensitive enough to pick this up. This does not mean that energy has not been moved or power acquired.

Wiccaning

A wiccaning is a ritual to present a child before the Goddess. You might say that it is an initiation into life, much like an initiation into witchcraft. The child is presented before divinity, blessed with the four elements and introduced to the powers that be; that these powers may recognize this child, acknowledge the child's humanity and connection to the ancestors, and protect this child on his/her journey through life.

Items needed:

1. White pillar wiccaning candle
2. Elemental candles for the quarters – green, yellow, red, and blue; I know these items fall under the title of 'general ritual tools' and would be included as a matter of course, but these candles have a special significance for this ritual and so I've listed them.
3. Small bowl of salt, placed at the north gate
4. Incense, placed at the east gate
5. Small bowl of water, placed at the west gate

The altar for a wiccaning can be decorated uniquely for each child and his/her family. This may include vintage photos of great-grandparents; family photos; flowers or herbs that have special familial associations; perhaps a stuffed animal or special doll or other toy passed down through the generations; a glass bowl filled with small strips of paper on which have been written special blessings and well-wishes for the child by friends and relatives. The ideas are endless.

The one item you want to have especially for the altar is a candle that you've chosen for this child. It should be white, and a nice pillar candle is recommended. Carve the child's name into this candle. A ribbon could be tied around the candle and other decorations added to it; a sticker can be placed on the bottom with the date of the wiccaning and other pertinent facts recorded here. The candle will become a keepsake.

As a preparation for this ritual, the parents should give the child a spiritually cleansing bath, which means 'bathing the child with intent'.

1. Cast the circle and call the quarters, but don't light the elemental candles yet.

2. Light your incense and the altar candle, 'The Mother Candle'.

3. Have the parents bring the child to the altar. Hold your hands over the child, saying:

'Upon this day we stand with this child, (name), before the Goddess, our ancestors, friends and family. We welcome this individual into the world and into this circle.'

4. Prepare to present the child to the Watchtowers at the four quarters. The Priestess and the parents, with the child, will stand before the north gate, the gate of Earth. Light the green elemental candle, and with your hand/wand/athame draw an invoking pentagram of Earth above it, saying:

'Watchtowers of the gate of Earth, we stand before you now to present to you this child, (name). By the power of Earth, bless (name) with physical health and material prosperity.'

Place a tiny pinch of salt upon the child's tongue.

Move to the east gate, the gate of Air. Light the yellow elemental candle, and with your hand/wand/athame draw an invoking pentagram of Air above it, saying:

'Watchtowers of the gate of Air, we stand before you now to present to you this child, (name). By the power of Air, bless (name) with wisdom, the agility of clear communication, and mental fortitude.'

Smudge the child with incense that is waiting at this gate and lit with the elemental candle.

Move to the south gate, the gate of Fire. Light the red elemental candle, and with your hand/wand/athame draw an invoking pentagram of Fire above it, saying:

'Watchtowers of the gate of Fire, we stand before you now to present to you this child, (name). By the power of Fire, bless (name) with a passion for justice and a lust for life.'

Carefully circle the child with the elemental candle.

Move to the west gate, the gate of Water. Light the blue elemental candle, and with your hand/wand/athame draw an invoking pentagram of Water above it, saying:

'Watchtowers of the gate of Water, we stand before you now to present to you this child, (name). By the power of Water, bless this child with intuition and an abundance of love in this life.'

Dip your fingers into the small bowl of water waiting for you at this gate and lightly sprinkle the child.

5. The Priestess and the parents, with the child, will move back before the altar.

The Priestess shall turn to the parents, saying:

'Who brings this child before the altar of the Goddess?'

The parents respond:

'We do.'

The parents will move forward to the altar and light the wiccaning candle, saying:

'It is our wish to bring (name) before the altar of the Goddess, that he/she may learn the Old Ways and walk the ancient Path.'

At this time, each parent, one after the other, may lay a token upon the altar that they've brought especially for this child – a pendant, a ring, a stone, an item that resonates with them, the child, and their family's energy. And while doing so, they may state – in their own words – a special blessing or wish for their child.

This is the perfect time to allow other family members present to become actively involved in the ritual by contributing a blessing, placing a token upon the altar, anointing the child's forehead with oil, or performing some other gesture of recognition and welcome. This could include grandparents, the child's siblings, aunts and uncles, etc.

6. The Priestess will step back before the altar. Raising her arms,

she'll say:

'This child, (name), has been acknowledged and blessed by the elements. We stand before the Goddess now and rejoice in the birth of this individual and the long journey of life to come. Goddess, touch this child with Your loving light.

The ritual is done.

So Mote It Be.'

7. Dismiss the quarters and dismantle the circle.

8. Celebrate this child's first footfall on life's journey.

Handfasting

Handfasting is not a legal marriage. It is a commitment between a couple to remain together for a year and a day. At the end of this time period, this relationship may be abandoned and the individuals will be free to go their separate ways, or the couple may decide to renew their handfasting vows and commit to each other for another year and a day.

The following ritual will give the couple a sense of commitment to their relationship and a chance to celebrate their union. A handfasting ritual will highlight the couple's bond of love to each other. It will bring blessings from the God and Goddess, and it will cement their relationship before family and friends.

Items needed:

1. Two white taper candles, one for each of the individuals being handfasted
2. Three ribbons, approximately 6 feet long, tied together in a knot at one end, preferably white, red, and black
3. Handfasting rings, or another piece of magical jewelry to be exchanged by the couple during the ritual
4. A handfasting broom, decorated as you wish for the occasion

The ritual:

1. The handfasting ritual may be performed inside a cast circle, with the quarters called. This would be the perfect opportunity to include the participation of friends or family members by assigning an individual to each of the four quarters, to invoke the element and light the elemental candle.

2. The Priestess will lay a broom near the altar, and she'll light the two white taper candles representing the couple, but not the main altar candle – this will be lit later during the ceremony. She'll also light the incense at this time.

3. The couple and the Priestess shall take their places, either in the center of the circle or before the altar, the couple standing together facing the Priestess. She will say:
   'We gather now in sacred space to witness the handfasting of this couple before the God and Goddess, before friends and family, and before the spirits of our ancestors.'

4. The Priestess speaks to the couple, saying:
   'You come today to publicly proclaim your commitment to each other. May you both walk the same path, but in doing so not lose sight of your own individuality and uniqueness. May you both walk the same path, but in doing so, respect each other's space and celebrate personal growth. May you walk the same path in love and light, reverence and joy.'

5. The Priestess says to the groom:
   'Do you come here freely, with love in your heart, to commit yourself to your partner?'

6. The groom responds:
   'I do.'

7. The Priestess says to the bride:

'Do you come here freely, with love in your heart, to commit yourself to your partner?'

8. The bride responds:

'I do.'

9. The Priestess now bids the couple to exchange their handfasting rings/jewelry; and at this time, the couple can take the opportunity to exchange personal vows of their own creation.

10. It's time for the couple to each take their lit taper candle and jointly light the white altar candle from these flames.

11. This point in the ceremony would also be the perfect time to include children or stepchildren in the ritual; either by giving them a commemorative pendant for the occasion, or allowing each child to light a personal candle on the altar to represent themselves and their bond with this couple...Personally, I think it would be lovely to include both of these suggestions.

12. The Priestess will then tell the couple to face each other and join their left hands, and as they do, she will take the bridal ribbons and, while wrapping them around the couple's wrists, she will say:

'By the power of the Goddess: the Maiden, the Mother, the Crone; and by the power of the God: the Green Man, the Horned God, the Sage, may your handfasting be blessed. You shall remain bound to each other for a year and a day. May your love grow and happiness flourish. So Mote It Be.'

13. The Priestess then removes the handfasting ribbons from the couple's wrists and lays them upon the altar. She may now

perform a 'cakes and wine' ritual, if this is to be included in the ceremony.

14. It's time now for the couple to 'jump the broom'. The Priestess may move the broom to the floor/ground before the altar. The couple will join hands and leap over it together.

15. The Priestess says:
'Over the broom and into your new life you leap.
Blessed Be!'

16. The ritual has ended; let the revelry begin!

Croning/Eldering

A croning is a ceremony that acknowledges a woman's passage into the third phase of life, honoring the third aspect of the Goddess. This ceremony usually takes place in a woman's life at the time of menopause.

This ritual is written for a group/coven setting, but it can be easily adapted for the solitary practitioner. When done as a group, two women will be chosen for the ceremony to represent the Goddess in her aspect of Maiden and Mother. These women can be coven sisters, or they may be the woman's relatives – mother, sisters, aunts, nieces.

Also, I want to mention that I have not written an eldering ceremony for a man; however, this ceremony could easily be adapted for this purpose. Simply start by changing the three aspects of the Goddess to the three aspects of the God: the Green Man, the Horned God, and the Sage.

Items needed:

1.   A black candle to represent the Crone
2.   A white taper candle for the Maiden and a holder for this candle

3. A red taper candle for the Mother and a holder for this candle
4. A special piece of jewelry, perhaps a pendant or a ring, that commemorates this occasion and will be presented as part of the ceremony

The altar will be decorated with those items which honor the Crone, the dark aspect of the Goddess. This will include the cauldron, and you will use this fireproof container to hold and burn the black candle for the ceremony. This cauldron will have a special place of honor in the center of the altar; place the holders for the two taper candles on either side of it.

A variety of herbs associated with the Crone, which could be laid about the altar to disperse energy, or burned as an offering, might include: anise, mugwort, elder, hazel, hellebore and tansy,[3] lilac, lavender, jasmine, ginger root, ash leaves/berries, blackberries, or thistle.

The stage is set, the ladies have gathered, the circle is cast and quarters called to witness this epic passage.

1. The Priestess stands before the altar, facing outward to the circle and the women gathered there. The woman about to experience the croning stands before the Priestess, facing her. The Priestess says:

'We invoke the Dark Mother. Upon this day we call forth the energy of the Crone, that we may be bathed in Her wisdom and experience, that we may embrace the shadows She casts, only to discover the light.'

2. The Priestess will then light the altar candles and the incense, but not the black candle, and come back to her place before the altar. The Priestess will say:

'Who comes today to represent this woman and her journey to this point?'

A young woman carrying a white unlit taper candle comes

forward before the Priestess; she says:

'I come forth to represent the path of Maiden, to represent beginnings, discoveries, and potential.'

The Priestess uses an altar candle to light the Maiden's white taper candle, which the Maiden then places in a holder on the altar. The Maiden takes her place to the left of the woman, standing by her side, facing the Priestess.

The Priestess says:

'Who comes today to represent this woman and her journey to this point?'

A woman in the midst of child-bearing age comes forward carrying an unlit red taper candle. She stops before the Priestess, saying:

'I come forth to represent the path of Mother, to represent fertility, strength, and purpose.'

The Priestess uses an altar candle to light the Mother's red taper candle, which the Mother then places in a holder on the altar. The Mother takes her place to the right of the woman, standing by her side, facing the Priestess.

As the three women stand facing the Priestess, the Priestess says:

'Who comes today to celebrate her journey to this point?'

The woman steps forward, saying:

'I do. I come forth to represent the Crone, to represent wisdom, experience, and accomplishment.'

The woman will then step to the altar and, using an altar candle, she will light the black candle that is sitting in the cauldron. The Crone will then return to her place between the Maiden and the Mother, where all three women will turn to face the circle and the ladies gathered there.

Now is the perfect time within the ceremony to include the participation of family or coven members, allowing individuals to come forward to embrace the new Crone and leave a flower upon the altar as an offering to the Goddess; as each individual passes through, they will then return to their place in the circle.

When this phase of the ceremony has been completed, the Maiden, Mother, and Crone will turn once more to face the altar and the Priestess. The Priestess says:

'You have forged your path in life. You have stood in the light and the shadows as well. To celebrate your arrival at this stage of life, you shall receive this token – blessed with the elements and infused with the energy of the Dark Mother.'

The Priestess then gives the woman her special piece of magical jewelry, either clasping a pendant around her neck, or placing a ring upon her finger.

The Priestess then says:

'May you continue upon your life path, walking it now as Crone, teaching the young ones the ways of the wise woman, spreading light upon those you love by embracing the shadows and the energy of the Dark Mother.

Blessed Be!'

The quarters will be dismissed, the circle dismantled.

Let the celebrations begin!

Summerland Ritual

The Pagan has a very different view of the afterlife than the Christian; and even within the Pagan community, you will find diverse beliefs about what happens to us when our bodies die. However you choose to look at death and what comes afterwards, the event itself will be marked, as all major events in a life generally are – with a ritual.

Items needed:

1. A white pillar candle representing the deceased
2. A photo of the individual

Besides the regular ritual tools, you will choose a white pillar candle to represent the deceased. You may want to carve the individual's name into it. This candle could also be adorned and decorated with herbs, sparkles, seashells, stones, ribbons, etc., or whatever else that resonates with the energy of the deceased – buttons from their clothing, beads from one of their necklaces.

The altar could also be decorated with flowers that were special to this individual, as well as personal items such as mementos from milestone occasions, old toys, things the individual may have collected, or items connected to an interest they pursued in life.

This ritual does not have to be conducted in a cast circle. However, the perimeter of the area could be set with white candles, white stones, bouquets of flowers, or bunches of herbs, and a purifying incense such as sandalwood.

1. When family and friends are gathered, the Priestess will stand before the altar, saying:

'As we all come from the Goddess to experience life; in death so shall we return to Her to experience peace.'

2. The Priestess will then light the altar candles, including the white pillar candle. Holding aloft the special white pillar candle, she will say:

'(name of deceased),

By the element of Earth, you were grounded in the physical world.

By the element of Air, you were open to knowledge and communication.

By the element of Fire, you were inspired with passion.

By the element of Water, you could dream your dreams.

So now, by Earth, by Air, by Fire, by Water…shall you pass to the next stage of your existence.'

3. The Priestess will then return the white candle to the altar. At this point, she may give a short eulogy on the deceased and his/her life; or family members and friends can be invited to come

forward and relate memories and stories.

4. A 'cakes and wine' ritual can be incorporated into the ceremony at this point, if the family members wish.

5. When these aspects of the ritual are complete, the Priestess will take her place at the altar, raise the white pillar candle before the assembled group, and say:
'(name of deceased),
Merry we meet,
And merry we part,
Until we merry meet again.'

6. The Priestess will then extinguish the flame of the white pillar candle. She may step forward and present this candle to the deceased's closest relative, spouse, or partner.

Part 3

Spells

Spells

It is assumed that you will create sacred space by casting a circle and calling the quarters before working magic, particularly magic that involves the darker energies. Even for those of you not seasoned in the practice of witchcraft, you should know that casting a circle is not that difficult. Go back to the previous sections of this book for more information, and you will find a circle casting listed with rituals.

Disposing of spells: After the ritual is complete and the magic cast, you are left with the remnants of your work — the ashes, candle wax, and other odds and ends. What do you do with it all? Depending upon what kind of spell these items sprang from, you will dispose of them in a variety of ways: you will bury it all off your property, or you will bury it on your property; you will throw it into running water; scatter it to the wind; place it in a mojo bag and put it in a special place, or perhaps carry the bag with you wherever you go. Throughout the instructions for most of these spells, I do believe I include how to dispose of the artifacts. If in doubt, you might listen to your own instinct: you're a wiser witch than you might think.

The spells listed here are all taken directly from my own Book of Shadows. I've carefully read through and decided upon a number of spells for a variety of intentions. I've chosen spells which have the spirit of the gray witch about them and that will fit with the energy of this book. Some of these spells are inspired by age-old traditions and others were birthed from my own imagination, desires, and intentions.

For those of you who don't have the heart of the gray witch, some of these spells might make you cringe; but you'll read transfixed, nevertheless, for the pull of the wild witch is strong within us all. Some of you have just tamed her, and others have allowed her to fly free.

Love Spells

I. Lilith's Lust Spell

This spell invokes Lilith, the notorious and unruly 'demon wife' of Adam. Her powerful and dominating sexuality is what caused their rift, and invoking the spirit of Lilith raises tremendous raw lust and sexual energy. A warning however – it isn't wise to invoke this entity in a home where there are newborn or young infants. Lilith's unquenchable appetite doesn't stop at sex.

Day: Friday
Hour: 1st/8th hour after sunrise; 3rd/10th hour after sunset
Planet: Venus
Moon Phase: waxing/full
Color: red
Herbs: for lust – cardamom; love and lust – ginseng; fidelity – a pinch of nutmeg, just to keep a leash on the energy being released
Oil: a sexuality oil or patchouli
Stone: pink quartz or blood stone
Symbols: the yin/yang symbol to highlight 'female/male' energy; I also intertwine the symbols for Mars and Venus – a mingling that radiates the energy of copulation
Deities: Lilith

First, you have to put yourself in the mindset for the type of energy you're going to receive from this spell. A long luxurious bath, satiny bold-colored lingerie, oils, and images...whatever it takes to arouse in you the heat of your own sexuality.

On a red candle carve the symbols and Lilith's name. Anoint the candle in oil and roll it in the combined herbs; set it up and light it and your incense as well. Music that throbs and gets you swaying and moving without thinking is wonderful for this moment. Begin to slowly move with it, closing your eyes, allowing the rhythm to fill you and sensations to wash over you.

Begin calling to Lilith, chanting to her, moving with her, feeling her in the pulsating rhythm of the music and your body. Lose yourself in the moment and in Lilith. When the energy climaxes and the peak is reached, you will know she has arrived. Make use of her energy for this night; she will leave as abruptly as she came.

2. Nutmeg Fidelity Spell
This spell uses nutmeg and its notorious reputation for inspiring fidelity. The use of intimate garments with the nutmeg is a form of sympathetic magic. Think well on this spell before you cast it – *remember that it will bind you into a mindset of fidelity just as much as it will bind your partner.*

Items needed:

1. Ground nutmeg
2. A red flannel bag that's large enough to hold two pairs of undergarments
3. A pair of your underpants and a pair of your partner's
4. A safety pin
5. A piece of parchment paper and a pen

On the parchment paper write your name and the name of your partner over the top of each other – spit on it. Fold this paper into a small square and place it in the red flannel bag. Take the undergarments and pin them together with a large safety pin, also placing them in the red flannel bag. To this bag sprinkle copious amounts of nutmeg; and, depending upon how squeamish you are, you could add a few drops of menstrual blood.

Keep this bag hidden in the bedroom. If your partner has occasion to be away for periods of time, on those occasions, take this bag into your bed and sleep with it.

3. Strawberry Sex Spell

If the passion in your relationship has waned and your partner is now moving on to greener pastures but you're not quite ready to let go yet, you can lure him back with this spell.

1. Choose a large scrumptious strawberry and sleep with it in your vagina for one night – preferably during a waxing moon.

2. You're going to have to be on decent terms with your partner in order to invite him for coffee or a meal. And during the course of this event, you will feed him a delectable dessert – perhaps a cupcake. The ingredients for this cake will be made with the minced strawberry that you slept with and, yes – a dash of nutmeg, as well as a generous sprinkling of powdered sugar – Drawing Powder.

The objective of this spell is to raise your partner's desire for you; to inspire lust, passion, and fidelity between the two of you; to make the idea of sex with someone else repulsive to your partner; and to lure your partner back to you – right where you feel he belongs.

4. Bloody Love Spell

It has long been believed that if a man ingests so much as a drop of a woman's menstrual blood, he will fall helplessly, hopelessly, eternally in love with her. (If you're squeamish at all – stop here now.)

This is considered a binding spell, as the gray witch knows, and it's considered the most potent love spell of all.

A word of warning: this is one spell that is almost impossible to reverse. You want to think long and hard before you cast this spell on your 'true love', because at some point in your life you may discover another love that seems even truer, and the monkey on your back will be a partner who is hopelessly caught under your enchantment. Also, be aware that the menstrual blood must be fed to the target *with magical intentions*!

In order to administer this blood, you must disguise it. Secrecy is what adds success to this spell; it is imperative in order for it to work. Traditionally a glass of red wine is the drink of choice; but it can also be hidden in a strong cup of coffee, a cola, or any other dark drink. The power and strength of this spell lie in the fact that the target will have no idea what hit him.

To add even more magical power, it would be best if the moon phase is waxing – or full, or as near to full as you can get. Friday, linked to the planet and the goddess Venus, will add strength to it as well, or an hour of the day influenced by Venus. Dates connected positively to your relationship are also energy boosters, such as an anniversary date.

5. Asunder You Shall Go: Dividing Lovers

This is a spell that will be inscribed on the photograph of a couple or on a name paper for the couple, if a photo is not available to you. It can be added to a mojo bag that you create for this couple to make their coupling miserable, or in a candle magic spell to put things into action. The gray witch knows that to fulfill her wishes, her creativity and imagination will provide endless possibilities.

1. On one side of the photograph (or the name paper) draw a dividing line down through the center of the couple, or between their names, preferably with black ink – or blood. When you do this, do it with purpose, intention, emotion, and power.

2. On the reverse side of the photo/paper, write the following verse:
    'This couple
    The spirits
    Shall divide
    With malice.'

6. The Face of Your True Love

It's believed that if you eat an apple on Samhain Eve and, without looking behind you, gaze into a mirror, you will see the face of your future husband or wife.

This might best be done in a darkened room lit with a single white candle, that shadows may fall, and secrets be revealed.

7. A Midsummer's Eve Love Spell

Upon the stroke of midnight at Midsummer's Eve, scatter rose petals about your garden, circling it thrice deosil (clockwise), while chanting or singing softly:

'Roses I strew,
True love to brew.
You'll find me,
So mote it be.
I'll find you,
Our love be true.'

Beauty

1. Shed Your Skin Spell

This spell takes advantage of the energy of three creatures who change or freshen their appearance by literally coming out in a new skin: the cicada, the moth or butterfly, and the snake. And you're going to be using in this spell one of three things: the abandoned skin of a cicada, the open and empty cocoon of a moth or butterfly, or the shed skin of a snake.

Shudder now and get over the 'ick' factor – real magic requires girding up your loins and getting your hands dirty once in a while – as the gray witch will tell you.

Day: Friday – associated with Venus, beauty, and love
Hour: 1st/8th hour after sunrise; 3rd/10th hour after sunset
Planet: Venus
Moon Phase: waxing to full

Color: pink, white, silver,

Herbs: for beauty – ginseng, lilac, rose; for youth – catnip, valerian

Oil: rose oil

Stone: rose quartz

Number: 6

Letters: f, o, x (no pun intended)

Symbols: The symbol for Venus

Deities: Venus/Aphrodite or Hathor

Items needed:

1. The dried shell of a cicada, an abandoned cocoon, or a snakeskin
2. A fireproof bowl
3. A bottle of rose oil
4. A pink or white candle
5. A red flannel bag

This spell works on the refreshing metamorphic energy of the creatures listed here. It also works on the mind and what you see, or what you think you see. This spell is not an instant facelift, but rather it changes the perception of how others view you and how you view yourself. It will give you the illusion of beauty and youth.

After the basic preparations are in place, the candles lit, the incense going, place upon your altar the fireproof bowl. Drop within it the insect skin, cocoon, or the snake shed and light it afire – you may need a bit of flammable oil sprinkled on the top to get it going.

When the fire has gone out and the remains have cooled off a bit, using your pestle, crush what's left into a pulp, adding a few drops of rose oil and drippings from your pink or white candle until you get a good consistency with a nice scent. Now take it in your hands – yes, in your hands – and roll it into a ball...drop this treasure in the red flannel bag.

Keep this bag in a secret spot, and on the evening of a full moon bring it out when you are alone in a darkened candle-lit room. Stand before a mirror, calling to the changing energy of the creature whose remains are in the bag. Wave the bag in a gentle back-and-forth motion before your face, saying:

'By the power of the creature here,
May youth and beauty shine pure and clear.
By the power of the creature within,
May I shed what's old to reveal fresh young skin.'

To Summon

1. Call Me

You're going to make a mojo bag for this spell. Create it during the waxing moon. The idea is to connect you and the person you wish to contact in a magical way with magical energy, thus manifesting your connection in the mundane world.

Items needed:

1. A photograph of each of you, or better yet, a photograph of the two of you together.
2. Two paperclips and/or glue.
3. A ribbon, the color of which will reflect your relationship with this person: red for a lusty passionate coupling, pink for friendship, white – which will cover any aspect, purple for soul sisters/brothers, green for business partners, etc.
4. A cloth bag, the color of which could reflect your intentions, just like the ribbon – it should be noted that red flannel is the traditional color and cloth for hoodoo magic.

If you're using two photos, glue them together, face to face, attach the paperclips to the four sides, and tie the photos together with the ribbon, making three knots, verbally embellishing each of these knots with your intentions.

If you're using one photo of the two of you, fold the photo in half so that you are face to face with this individual. Glue the photo together, paper clip the edges, and tie it up with the ribbon, making three knots – stating your intentions loud and clear to the universe as you go.

Drop this photo in your bag. Keep it in a safe place until you make contact, after which, this bag can either be kept to insure continued interaction with this person, or it can be burned and the ashes scattered to the wind – insuring open communication through the element of Air.

2. Summoning Powder

You're going to create this powder and use it in a variety of ways to summon to you a particular person. You will sprinkle this powder on a piece of clothing you may have that belongs to the target; on correspondence that you've saved, or on a new piece of correspondence you're mailing out; on the target's property – their doorstep, the walk before their house, etc. – in secret, of course.

However, a safer method, and one which doesn't have the potential of getting you into trouble, would be to put the target's photo, signature, or name paper in a red flannel mojo bag and add summoning powder to it. You keep the bag, and you decide what to do with it and when. This also gives you absolute control over the spell, the target, and the outcome – I like this option best.

Crush and blend the following three ingredients, of equal amounts, in your mortar with a pestle:

Bay leaves
Cinnamon
Anise

To this succulent mound of herbs, add Drawing Powder (powdered sugar) – in an amount equal to the batch of herbs you've just crushed.

Voilà...Summoning Powder.

3. Rosemary Summons

Use rosemary and a pinch of Drawing Powder to summon someone to you that you have feelings for, or whose help you need. This could include someone you have romantic feelings for; someone you love in a platonic way; someone that you're connected to through blood or circumstance; or someone whose help you need with an issue or personal problem. Think of this spell as a pied piper's wiggling finger inferring, *'Come hither.'*

You will gather a handful of dried rosemary, a photo/signature/or name paper of the one you need to summon, and a lovely little fire – either outdoors in a nice fire pit, or a smaller adaptation in your cauldron.

When you get your fire burning properly, drop into it the photo/signature/or name paper; next, the rosemary, sprinkling it carefully so you don't smother your flames. And finally, just a pinch of Drawing Powder.

As the flames consume the ingredients of your spell, chant:
'Blessed rosemary, I call unto thee;
Summon (name) to come to me.'

4. To Beckon

This is a very gentle spell – yes, the gray witch embraces this type of magic, contrary to popular belief. The purpose of this spell is to give a subtle suggestion to someone you wish to have contact with. This is not an in-your-face summons, but a soft tap on the shoulder; and this spell does not force anyone to do anything they do not wish to do. If the person to whom you beckon likes the feel of the energy you send their way, they will respond.

This spell is all about energy, and that's all you will use in the casting of it.

Find a peaceful comfortable spot to plant yourself, either outdoors in the midst of nature, or in a space that you've structured for yourself to be conducive to meditation and concentrated thought – perhaps complete with soft background music (instrumentals only), candles, and incense.

When you have centered and grounded yourself and cleared your mind of disruptive chatter, home in on the person you will be sending this energy to. Close your eyes and visualize their face before you; as you do, chant softly either their name – over and over in a mesmerizing sing-song chant, or you can repeat these words:

'Know I call to you,
Think of me,
Think of me,
So Mote It Be.'

You will continue chanting until you feel the energy build and roll, and when it has become overwhelming, send it off. Release it with a breath, with a hand gesture, with a sigh or a shout. If you've never done this type of spell casting before, you will come to recognize very quickly the feeling of building energy. Sometimes it has actually given me butterflies in my tummy, as though I were moving. And you will know when you've thrown it out into the world; it will often leave your space in a 'whoosh' that sends goose bumps rushing up your legs.

5. Summoning Spirits

For this summoning spell, we're going to use Black Cat Oil. Not only is this oil a powerful conduit for summoning spirits; it's also often used to break bad spells, and for protection. This oil will contain a pinch of hair from a black cat – the most important ingredient.

Contrary to popular myth, black cats do *not* bring bad luck.

They are said to be a favorite form for shape-shifting spirits; and this is one reason it's considered bad luck to harm a black cat – that purring beautiful ball of fur before you might in fact be a magical creature or spirit who is observing you just as keenly as you are observing it.

Black cats are thought to have special magical connections and have long been a favored creature for a witch's familiar.

First, the Black Cat Oil.

Items needed:

1. Herbs: sage, bay leaves, myrrh – substitutions for myrrh include anise, cloves, lemon balm, and cinnamon
2. Steel wool
3. Iron
4. Black cat hair
5. Oil – for the base: castor oil for protection, as well as to break curses/hexes/spells; almond oil, to attract the opposite sex

Mix these ingredients together and warm them in your cauldron, just until you smell the herbs, knowing that the energy is released. Add this mixture to a jar, and leave it to sit for a night beneath the moonlight.

To summon spirits:

Anoint a blue or purple candle with Black Cat Oil and burn this candle, calling in the spirits.

To summon a particular spirit, such as a loved one who's passed, I create an altar for this spirit filled with photos, favorite personal items, a piece of clothing having belonged to them in life, etc. Samhain evening would be the most advantageous time to perform a ritual such as this, but you can call spirits to you at any time you desire them.

Health and Healing

I. Basic Candle Spell and Correspondences
Day: Thursday

Hour: 1st/8th hour after sunrise; 3rd/10th hour after sunset

Planet: Jupiter

Moon Phase: waxing/full, to bring good health; waning/dark, to banish illness

Color: green

Herbs: health – rosemary, sage, St. John's Wort; healing – garlic, fennel, thyme

Oil: Health and Healing Oil

Incense: lavender or sandalwood

Stone: green jasper, jade, mossy agate, blue-lace agate

Number: 3

Letters: c, l, u

Symbols: rune 'sigil', for healing; rune 'uruz', for physical health; triple ring

Deities: Horus

When your sacred space is created and secure, your candle anointed and rolled in the appropriate herbs, write this spell upon a piece of parchment or paper. Recite it three times, and burn it in the flame of your spell candle – scattering the ashes to the wind to dispose of it.

'I cast now a healing spell for (name),
That there shall be unto thee,
Blessings of good health and healing,
By the power of three times three,
So Mote It Be.'

2. To Cure an Illness (knot magic)
Traditionally knot magic is done with a 9-foot-long red cord or ribbon. But for this healing spell, we're going to use the healing

energy of the color green. Make sure that you mark nine points on your green cord or ribbon, where nine knots will be tied.

The idea behind knot magic is that we tie up our intentions, as well as the energy that can manifest those intentions, within the knot. For this spell, we're going to grab the energy to banish illness on the night of the dark moon, or within three nights afterwards. We'll cast the spell, tie the knots, and lay this cord aside to let the magic ferment. As the energy of the moon grows and builds towards the full moon, so does the energy contained within the knots. On the night of the full moon, we will untie each knot, unleashing the magic and manifestation.

Items needed:

1. A 9-foot-long green cord/ribbon
2. Three votive candles – two black, one green
3. White pillar altar candle
4. Health and Healing Oil
5. A blue-lace agate stone
6. A red flannel bag

Assuming your space is prepared, your circle cast and quarters called, you will carve the name of the target on the green candle and anoint it with the Health and Healing Oil. Line the three votive candles up on your altar, the green candle being in the center. Light all your altar candles and incense, and get yourself seated and comfortable to work on your knots.

As you tie the knots, keep an image of the target before you on your altar, preferably a photograph, or an image visualized in your mind, if you don't have a picture.

Tie each knot to the following chant, and as you work from knot to knot, keep the chant going continuously. Take your time. Eventually the chant may run together in a whispered frenzy. It also may become very mesmerizing, and you may feel 'floaty' and spacey by the time you reach the end of the ribbon. This is good; it means that you've put yourself in an alpha state, where magic is possible.

The chant:

'Illness leave, go away,
Good health I bid you come to stay.'

When the knots are tied, the chanting stopped, and the candle has burned down, add the ribbon, the blue-lace agate, and the remains of the candle wax to the red flannel bag. You can keep this bag on your altar till the full moon, if possible; if not, make sure you put it in a safe place till the time is ripe.

On the night of a full moon, you will seat yourself within a cast circle, and by the light of a white altar candle, you will begin to slowly untie the knots, releasing the magic. As you do so, chant the chant:

'I open now the healing gates;
Good health upon the one who waits,
(name).'

All the remnants of this spell – the ribbon, bag, stone, candle wax – can be disposed of by either burying it in the earth, or burning everything and scattering the ashes to the wind.

3. Healing Crystal

I love the energy of crystals and stones, and I work with them often. I surround myself, my home, and my very person with this special magic. One very positive thing you can do to generate a warm and healing atmosphere in your home is to choose a crystal that resonates with you, bless it for healing and peace, and place it in an auspicious location in your house or apartment.

First, you'll have to choose a crystal – and this can be a delightful adventure and project in itself. Browse shops, taking your time. Look at as many crystals as you need to. Hold them, handle them, until a particular crystal seems to call to you. After finding this treasure and purchasing it, you will take it home and bless it: holding the crystal in your hands, you will imbue it with your energy and intentions, feeling it warm as the energy is absorbed. Take your time during this process, and enjoy.

You can use an altar to bless this crystal, making the process as ritualistic and detailed as you wish, or you can simply continue with just you and the stone.

If you have a patron god or goddess, call upon their energy to bless this stone, along with the vibrational tone from your own environment and the energy of your body, coupled with the will of your intentions. State aloud and clearly exactly what type of energy you wish this crystal to emanate, focusing on this type of energy, visualizing it moving through your body, your arms, down to your hands and into the crystal itself.

This crystal will sit in a special place, where its energy can spread and radiate throughout your living quarters. Every once in a while, if you feel the need, you can recharge this crystal, or you can cleanse it by holding it beneath running water, leaving it briefly in a bowl of sea salt, letting it sit beneath the moonlight – or in the sunlight – depending upon which energy you wish to work with.

Command and Compel Spells

1. Commanding Oil
This is the basic recipe I use, from my own Book of Shadows, to create a Commanding Oil; and this recipe has worked successfully for me.

Items needed:

Herbs: calamus root and licorice root – other plants with strong commanding properties may include vetiver and bergamot, which is a good commanding herb for matters pertaining to finances
Oils: you can use – as a base – olive oil, baby oil (unscented), or mineral oil; for a commanding oil of malevolent intentions, use castor oil

Combine and crush your chosen herbs in a mortar and pestle, add them to the oil. Either heat the oil in a pot just until you begin to smell the herbs, releasing their energy, and pour it into a jar; or add the oil and herbs directly to a jar and leave it to sit beneath the sun or the moon for several hours.

It's that simple.

2. Do My Bidding Spell

In order to get another person to bend to your will and do what you want, you will create a candle spell using Commanding Oil. You will, in essence, put yourself *above* your target, overpowering them magically, allowing the oil to do its work.

Items needed:

1.   One black candle to represent your target
2.   One white candle to represent yourself
3.   Commanding Oil
4.   Three straight pins

Carve the name of your target on the black candle and anoint this candle with Commanding Oil. Insert three straight pins an equal distance apart about an inch from the top of the candle. Carve your own name on the white candle. You will situate these candles so that the white candle representing you is above the black candle representing your target. I've actually taken a small slip of paper and written on it exactly what I wanted the target to do, folding it and slipping it beneath the black candle.

You will situate these candles so that the white candle is positioned *above* the black candle. As the black candle burns down, the straight pins will eventually begin to fall, and as they do, so too, the will of your target will crumble.

Take the remnants of this spell and bury them in the earth.

Court Case Spells

1. Basic Candle Spell and Correspondences

Day: Thursday

Hour: 1st/8th hour after sunrise; 3rd/10th hour after sunset

Planet: Jupiter

Moon Phase: waxing to bring something to you; waning to send something away

Color: purple (power), brown (justice), green (for money issues)

Herbs: for the energy of Jupiter – cinnamon, nutmeg, sage; for legal affairs – marigolds; for justice – bay; to fight false accusations and testimony – slippery elm

Oil: Commanding Oil, or Court Case Oils

Powders: Drawing Powder – to draw something to you; Banishing Powder, to send something away

Incense: sandalwood; for more aggressive magic – patchouli

Stone: tiger eye

Number: 8

Letters: h, q, z

Symbols: The rune 'thurisa' – neutralizes your enemies and protects; Earth – protects the person whose name you write within; Odin's Cross

The most basic court case candle spell is as follows:

1. Get yourself the appropriately colored candle for your situation. Hold this candle in your hands and charge it with your intentions – and this is one of those times you might want to be extremely specific.

2. Carve upon this candle those symbols, names, amounts, or dates that may be pertinent to your case. Dress this candle with the oil you feel will do you the most good – and it may not be just

those listed here – and then roll the candle in a combination of the crushed herbs.

3. You can write out your desires for the type of outcome you're looking for on a piece of paper and burn it in the flame of this candle. Allow this candle to burn itself out and then bury the remains of this spell *off* your property to send something away; bury it *on* your property to bring something to you.

2. Magical Options for Legal Spells

If money is your issue, make sure you use money in your spells, whether you feel compelled to burn it, bury it, or throw it in a stream of running water.

If someone's negativity or bad behavior is playing a large part in your legal situation, pull out the big guns and bind them – with knot magic, poppets, Commanding Oil and spells, or anything else it takes to put you in charge and help you regain control.

If the judge in your case is the one making the final call, target him/her, going right to the heart of the matter to manipulate the outcome.

3. Beef Tongue Court Case Spell

This quaint little spell is steeped in hoodoo tradition, and if you are squeamish, it could be a bit of a challenge. I have actually had the pleasure of using this delightful twisted magical gun when I was going through the legal proceedings of a nasty divorce and had reached the point where I'd had enough. Of course, right in the midst of the best part of the spell, our neighbor lady knocked on the backdoor. My girls practically bowled her over to keep her out of the house so I could finish the job. This spell will work for you, I can tell you this from personal experience, so stick with it and see it through – make the gray witch proud.

Items needed:

1. A raw beef tongue (you should be able to find this in the meat department of your local grocery store)
2. Several slips of paper and a pen
3. Pins and needle and thread
4. A strip of red flannel cloth large enough to wrap up the tongue
5. Cayenne pepper
6. Four Thieves Vinegar

Make sure you have a decent place to work where you'll have plenty of room to spread things out and get comfortable; this may take a while.

1. Begin by writing on these small slips of paper the names of the judge, the attorneys, adversaries, witnesses, and anyone connected to your case who may have a negative impact or influence upon it or you – one name per slip!

2. Using a sharp knife, cut small slits into the beef tongue – a slit for each slip of paper.

3. Insert one name paper into each slit.

4. Sprinkle the tongue with cayenne pepper and Four Thieves Vinegar.

5. Close the slits in the tongue with straight pins, or do what I did – sew the slits shut with needle and thread.

6. Wrap the tongue in red flannel and place it in your freezer while the court case is in progress. When you've reached the end of this ordeal and all is said and done, remove the tongue from your freezer and bury it in the earth.

The Gray Witch's Grimoire

Money Spells

1. Basic Candle Spell and Correspondences
Day: Thursday
Hour: 1st/8th hour after sunrise; 3rd/10th hour after sunset
Planet: Jupiter
Moon Phase: waxing – to bring money; waning – to banish poverty or debt
Color: green
Herbs: basil, cloves, mint – money; nutmeg – prosperity; dill – for financial matters regarding children
Oil: Prosperity Oil or patchouli
Incense: patchouli
Stone: aventurine
Number: 3
Letters: c, l, u
Symbols: the rune 'fehu' (material wealth/possessions); triple ring, triformis

Note: It's advantageous to use 'Drawing Powder' in money spells. I do.

Using the correspondences above, set up your space to do a candle spell, decorating an altar with handfuls of coins; paper money; tokens of prosperity; images of deities that draw abundance; symbols listed above; and anything else that represents 'money' and 'prosperity' to you. Get your patchouli incense going, and then take a green candle, anoint it with the appropriate oil and roll it in crushed herbs. (Of the herbs listed, mint is the main one I use for money spells.) Write your intentions on a slip of paper and burn it in the flame of the candle. Dispose of the remnants in a manner most fitting to your situation.

You can also use the correspondences above to create a money mojo bag – and be sure to add to this bag coins and paper money. (Like attracts like, remember.)

144

2. Money Bottle

Witches' Bottles are a popular old form of magic. A bottle is filled with herbs and a variety of other objects connected to an intention. Witches' Bottles are, in essence, a spell sealed within a glass container. In order to bring this magic into fruition, you can do several things with the bottles – some may be buried on your property, depending upon what kind of spell is involved; they can be placed in a conspicuous spot inside your house, like by the front door, and given a gentle little 'shake' every now and then to keep the energy alive; or they can be hidden in your home, in a secret spot, so only you know that magic is afoot.

We're going to create a witches' bottle here that will send positive energy our way for wealth and prosperity. Items needed:

1. A nice-sized bottle with a lid
2. A pinch or handful of rice, dill, and/or poppy seeds – along with a nice batch of mint
3. A stone of aventurine
4. Patchouli oil
5. Coins and a dollar bill

Upon the dollar bill, write in green ink:

'Magic build within this glass,
Riches flow and come to pass;
Money magic work for me,
As I do will, So Mote It Be.'

After you deposit all of the ingredients in your bottle, screw on the lid and seal it with green wax from your charged candle. Recite this chant as you shake up the bottle and its contents.

Your money bottle can be kept somewhere in your home where it's close by and handy and you can shake it up every once in a while to reactivate and ignite the energy within; or you can bury your money bottle somewhere on your property, to work in secret.

3. Keep It Flowing

This is another spell based on hoodoo tradition – gotta love it. It's one of those money spells that won't make you filthy rich, but it will protect you from running out of money for life's essentials. (One of these days I'll come up with a spell to make us filthy rich; until then, this will have to do.)

Items needed:

1. A small bowl or a decorative container that resonates with your own energy
2. Salt
3. Drawing Powder
4. Rice
5. Crushed mint leaves
6. An open safety pin – for this spell I could also suggest, in place of a safety pin, a brooch that you will leave open, unclasped. This could be something that resonates with the idea of money – or in my case I used a brooch that had belonged to my grandmother, a deceased family member who loved me and who would want me to have all that I needed, a family member who would help me in life any way that she could, and who will help me from the spirit world.

Fill your bowl or open container with a handful or pinch of each of the ingredients listed above, depending on the size of your receptacle, usually an equal amount of every ingredient used. Within the center, place the unclasped safety pin or brooch. If you've used a brooch that belonged to a family member, it would be a good idea to include an invocation to this spirit, as well as a thank-you for their help.

Keep this bowl in an open place within your home, and when you feel it needs it, refresh the ingredients; perhaps at regular intervals, such as every third full moon.

Spells for the Tongue

1. A Poppet to Stop a Gossip

Items needed:

1. Black cloth
2. Cotton balls
3. Needle and thread (black)
4. Herbs: patchouli, cloves, pepper, wormwood, and any other 'binding' herbs of your choice
5. A black onyx stone
6. A safety pin
7. Straight pins
8. Pen and paper
9. A red flannel bag large enough to hold the poppet, and black ribbon to tie it shut
10. Cemetery dirt (optional, but highly suggested)

You're going to make a black poppet, a dolly representing the individual who is spreading malicious gossip and lies about you. And if you think you can't sew, think again. If you can thread a needle and sew a stitch, you can make a poppet.

1. Double your material and cut out a rough rudimentary human shape. This will give you the front and back of your poppet. You can draw this figure on a sheet of paper first, cutting this out and using it as a guide, if you wish.

2. Sew the two pieces of cloth together, but don't sew it entirely

closed until you have added the herbs, the stone, cemetery dirt, a photograph of your target, a name paper, or other personal effects from this individual. Fill the dolly with cotton balls to flesh it out, then you can either leave a safety pin in the side, so you can reopen it to add something once in a while, or you can finish sewing it shut.

3. Ideally, you will have a photo of this person that you can print off and cut out to fit the face of the poppet. Glue or pin it on the dolly and then stick straight pins through the mouth, slowly, with intention, talking to the image if you wish, telling them just what you think of their falsehoods and innuendos. You can create a blindfold for the eyes by cutting out a small strip of material and tying it around the dolly's head, so they'll be blinded in their ambition to destroy your reputation and good name.

4. As a devious, devilish finale, you can plant this dolly head first in a flowerpot full of cemetery dirt, leaving the legs sticking straight in the air; perhaps growing a nice lush binding herb around it, such as wormwood.

I'll bet this spell will make most people think twice about spreading gossip and tarnishing someone's good reputation. This spell contains the *cringe factor*. I can almost hear Karma sigh with finality and the gray witch giggle in delight.

2. Seal the Mouth Spell

This spell works very much on the premise of the previous spell, only we're not going to use a poppet – we're going to use an enlarged photo of our target.

For this spell, cast the circle widdershins (counterclockwise) for dark magic, being sure to call the quarters to stand guard.

Items needed:

1.   A photo of your target, enlarged so that it will be easy to

work with; 8″ x 10″ works best
2.   Sewing needle and black thread
3.   Goofer Dust
4.   Black candle
5.   Cloves
7.   Banishing Oil or Commanding Oil, depending upon your intentions

Hidden away in a darkened room, by the flickering light of candles – including the black spell candle, oiled and dressed with Goofer Dust and cloves, burning with intention and magic – you will take up the photo of the target and, dipping your fingertip in oil, anoint the picture with the banishing pentagrams of Earth, Air, Fire, and Water.

Across this photograph, in the witches' alphabet, write:

'I do seal your mouth
and silence your voice,
So you shall hear
The dark angels rejoice.'

Take up the needle and thread, and very carefully sew the target's mouth shut, chanting the spell as you sew, ranting and throwing curses towards this person. Watch the eyes of the target in the photograph: you may see a dawning change come over them – a sense of panic or 'knowing' that comes through the image. It's as though the individual has a sudden realization of what is happening to them.

You can do a couple of things with the photo:

You can set the photo on your altar near the cauldron while the candle burns itself out, talking to the image, chanting to it, watching the glow of the flames play across the face. Then bury the remnants of the candle left in the cauldron, and keep the photograph where you can pull it out from time to time for use in other spells towards this target, or when you just want to 'bother' it a bit, giving the target no rest.

The alternative is that you can chant the spell until the energy builds, and then set this photograph alight by the flame of the black candle, allowing it all to burn itself out. Bury everything in the cauldron, candle remnants as well as the ashes from the photo, *off* your property.

You might as well have the target's tongue hanging from a hook – they will no longer be able to speak ill of you, to spread lies and gossip about you, or to harass you with their speech in any way.

3. Cat's Got Your Tongue Spell

You have to find out if someone is telling you the truth, or if they are lying to you. This spell will do just that.

Items needed:

1. A candle, the color of which will suit your situation – green for money/business issues, red for relationships, or white to cover anything else
2. Herbs of your choice, to suit your situation – mint for money or business, rose petals for relationships, and sage to cover anything else
3. Several strands of different-colored thread and string
4. The hair from a cat – just a snippet will do
5. A small red flannel bag to hold it all, and make sure this bag is small enough to fit in your pockets

Prepare your space, dress the candle and light it – and some incense as well. I can't do anything without a bit of incense going; it clears the way.

As the candle flickers and burns, take the thread and strings, dropping them in a delightful colored heap before you, tossing them gleefully, as you would toss a salad, deliberately tangling them, chanting the entire time:

'*Oh, what a tangled web you weave,*

When you deliberately choose to deceive.'

When the energy is raised and released, the candle burned down, and your chanting has stopped, place the candle wax, the tangled string, and the cat's hair in the small red flannel bag.

Carry this bag on your person, in your pocket, as you go to finish what you've started. Confront the target then, asking them the question for which you seek an honest answer. If this individual is telling you the truth, their words will be clear and strong; if they are lying to you they will stutter, splutter, slur their words and fall over their own tongue...because the cat will have it.

4. Keep My Secret

Did you go and tell someone your deepest darkest secret, and now you're afraid they are going to spill the beans? Have no fear; you can make them keep it.

Items needed:

1. An enlarged photo of your target
2. Parchment or paper and a pen
3. Scissors and glue
4. Candles, incense, and oils of your choosing

First, create your sacred space, setting the mood. How inspiring to work by the flickering flames of magical candles, with the essence of your favorite incense spicing the air!

On the parchment paper, write out the secret that must be kept. If this can be set to paper in just a few short words, write small and cut it out. You're going to take this piece of paper and glue it onto the photo, over the mouth of your target. If your secret requires a lot of writing, perhaps even the whole page, you will glue the entire page over the photograph of your target, virtually smothering them with the secret and freezing the knowledge in place – it will go no further.

Allow the glue to dry, then place this photo in a safe place where it will remain undisturbed for as long as the secret must be kept. If the day comes when silence is no longer necessary, take the photo from its hiding place, burn it in the flame of a white candle, and scatter the ashes to the wind, effectively releasing the target from their bond of silence.

5. Liar Come to Light Spell

Are you involved in a social situation, or perhaps a business transaction, with a group of people, and you think that someone may be lying to you? You're not sure, you don't have proof – just a feeling, and you have to know. If this is the situation you find yourself in, this is your spell.

Items needed:

1. A white votive candle
2. Eight straight pins
3. A sheet of paper and a pen

Draw a dividing line on the paper, right through the center. On one side of this paper, write 'yes'; on the other side of the paper, write 'no'. Take the candle, and about one inch from the top, begin inserting the straight pins. Continue placing these pins around the candle an equal distance from each other and *at the same level*.

Place this candle in the center of the paper, so that it's situated on the line you drew. Half of the candle will be over the positive side of the paper (yes), and the other half of this candle will be over the negative side of this paper (no).

Light the candle and prepare to settle in to watch the flame. As you do this, you may become very relaxed, even entering an alpha state; and you could be surprised at the psychic revelations revealed. However, don't become so relaxed or distracted that you forget to watch the candle. The first needle to fall will give you your answer: yes or no.

Protection Spells

1. Basic Candle Spell and Correspondences
Day: Saturday

Hour: 1st/8th hour after sunrise; 3rd/10th hour after sunset

Planet: Saturn

Moon Phase: waxing – to bring protection to you; waning – to banish whatever you need protection from

Color: black

Herbs: fennel, mint, sage, thistle, nightshade (poisonous),[4] black pepper, cayenne pepper, garlic, dill (especially protects children)

Oil: Banishing Oil or Mars Astrological Oil (good stuff)

Incense: sandalwood

Stone: obsidian, red jasper

Number: 8

Letters: h, q, z

Symbols: Earth symbol – write the name of who or what you want protected within it

Deities: Brigit (when seeking protection for children)

Using the correspondences above, set up your sacred space, dress your candle with oil and the herbs. What exactly is it that you feel you need protection from? If it's an individual and you are fortunate enough to have their photo in your possession, place it on a small mirror and circle it with salt and graveyard dirt, trapping them within. Burn the spell candle near this image. If it's a situation, create a mojo bag using these correspondences and the remains of your spell candle, inserting into the bag those items connected in some way with the troublesome situation or people involved.

2. A Vehicle Blessing

We used to make quite a few road trips with the family when the children were small, and before each new adventure, I would bless our vehicle to keep the occupants safe from an accident. I still do this periodically, not only with my own vehicle, but with my children's vehicles, when I can get my hands on them.

The following blessing can be performed in conjunction with creating a mojo bag to hang in your vehicle or to conceal beneath the seat, its purpose being to keep you safe and prevent accidents. I included a spell for this bag in my first book, *Tarot: A Witch's Journey*. You can perform this little ritual in the privacy of your enclosed garage, which I've done several times; or you can brave the neighbors' curiosity by performing this ritual in your driveway, which I've also done several times.

The Correspondences

Note: You should know that I've had to modify the timing for this ritual on several occasions, in accordance with our travel plans, and that will work just fine. Also, if you have herbs that you personally work with for protection spells and that work for you, feel free to substitute them for this ritual. Below are the correspondences I use from my own Book of Shadows.

Day: Tuesday

Hour: 1st/8th hour after sunrise; 3rd/10th hour after sunset

Planet: Mars

Moon Phase: preferably waxing to full

Color: black or orange

Herbs: dill, fennel, rosemary, plantain (use dill especially for the protection of children)

Oil: Mars Astrological Oil or a good protection oil of your choosing

Incense: sandalwood

Stone: black obsidian, red jasper, citrine, tiger eye

Symbol: the planetary symbol for Mars, and the symbol for

Earth, as well as the invoking pentagram for Earth

Items needed:

1. Six candles: green (Earth), yellow (Air), red (Fire), blue (Water), white (Spirit), black – for the cauldron
2. Your oil and incense
3. Small bowl of water and salt
4. Parchment or paper on which you've written the spell you'll find below
5. Any of the herbs that you care to use in a mojo bag, to use in the ritual, or to place within the vehicle

Arrange the elemental candles around the vehicle in the pattern of a pentagram. If you're pinched for space, you can even arrange them upon the hood of the vehicle. Light the candles and the incense. Have the black spell candle dressed in oil and herbs and placed within your cauldron, or a fireproof receptacle. Light it as well. Using your oil, go around the vehicle and anoint the front, the back, the tires, and each of the doors with the oil, using the invoking pentagram for Earth.

I open the door and, with my bowl of salted water in hand, I asperge the interior of the vehicle. I've also been known to throw a dash of sea salt here and there, as well as some crushed sage.

Go then to the front of the vehicle, before the white candle of spirit and your cauldron containing the burning black spell candle. Recite the spell below out loud, following the directions as you do so, and then burn the written spell in the flame of your spell candle, allowing the ashes to mingle with the melted wax. This can all be used later by adding it to your mojo bag.

The spell:

'I cast now a spell to protect
All those who will occupy this space,
Creating for them a sacred place.

'I bless this vehicle by the powers of Earth.'

(walk in a complete circle around your vehicle, carrying a bowl of salt, stopping before your cauldron candle)

'I bless this vehicle by the powers of Air.'

(walk in a complete circle around your vehicle, carrying the burning incense, stopping before your cauldron candle)

'I bless this vehicle by the powers of Fire.'

(walk in a complete circle around your vehicle, carrying the burning white candle of spirit, stopping before your cauldron candle)

'I bless this vehicle by the powers of Water.'

(walk in a complete circle around your vehicle, carrying the bowl of water, stopping before your cauldron candle)

'As these elements protect and guard my magic circle,

So shall they protect and guard all those who ride within this vehicle.

I empower this spell three times three,

As I do will, So Mote It Be.'

Gently lower the written spell to the flame of the black candle, igniting the parchment, and drop it into the cauldron to finish burning. Extinguish the elemental candles, but allow the black spell candle to burn itself out. Dismantle your circle, if you have cast one, and eat something to ground yourself. I've found that this spell can be quite draining for some reason, so don't neglect the last suggestion; and don't be surprised if you are very hungry at the end of it.

3. To Spite Your Face

One of the most frustrating foes to deal with is a person who is jealous and spiteful. This spell will deal with their energy, while most importantly, it will protect you from the fallout of their actions and their spitefulness.

Items needed:

1. A cauldron containing a nice little pile of burning herbs (slippery elm and sage would be nice, but sage will do), creating a respectable-sized flame – you might want to use a small charcoal tablet, just to keep things going
2. A black votive candle
3. A photo of the target – if this is not available, their signature or a name paper will have to do
4. A red flannel bag
5. Three blossoms from a thorny plant, preferably a thistle; or three thorns – which are just as effective

Carve the target's name on the black spell candle, and set it on your altar, near your cauldron. Light it – with glee and delight, knowing that you are lighting a flame beneath your enemy's feet.

You will take their photo and, with the focused emotions you feel at this person and their actions, you will mark it, slash it, spit on it, stomp on it – or do something else even more dastardly to it, all the while maintaining the focus and intent of your actions. *It's imperative that you do not lose sight of your intentions.*

Burn this image in your cauldron, amidst the herbs and flames.

When the fire has burned down, the black candle has burned itself out, and everything has cooled down – except your emotions and will – deposit the ashes and remnants of this spell into the red flannel bag.

Then add three blossoms or three thorns to the bag, one at a time.

With the first blossom/thorn, say:
'The first I add to freeze your speech.'
With the second blossom/thorn, say:
'The second I add to halt your reach.'
With the third blossom/thorn, say:
'The third I add to spite your face,
That you may wallow in disgrace.'

Keep this bag in a safe and secret place, allowing the magic time to mature and ripen, that the target will feel the full effects.

4. The In-Law Spell

I have experienced within my lifetime the effects of one of the relationships that can be the most poisonous and destructive – in-laws. These people don't have to have a reason for disliking you; your existence is usually good enough reason. If you've reached what you feel is 'the point of no return' and contact with these people is proving destructive to your family and overly stressful, or even harmful to your health, it's time to bid them farewell. No, we're not going to harm them, or banish them; we're just going to mark our territory and let the power of magic make it off limits to them.

Think of a tomcat and how he marks his territory. Basically we're going to do the same thing, but without the urine. Instead, we're going to use the magic of the green witch to mark our space with the herb *oregano*.

You're going to want a good-sized hefty cast-iron cauldron, some charcoal tablets to keep things going, and a plentiful quantity of oregano. You are going to get a good handful of oregano burning in your cauldron, and then tone it down so that it's smoldering and smoking up a storm. And no, you probably won't like the smell of it – but it works like a charm – pun intended! The essence of the oregano will magically keep your in-laws at bay.

Carry this cauldron throughout your home, smudging every room, and most importantly – *every entrance!* And I do mean *every* entrance: garage doors, back doors, old cellar doors you haven't used in ages, portals, doggy doors, and windows – any opening into your home – *smudge it!*

You should also smudge a photograph of these in-laws. To add fuel to my fire, so to speak, I actually burned a photograph of them in my cauldron so that it was smoldering away with the oregano.

It's been years since I performed this unique and useful little spell...and it's been years since my threshold has seen the shadow of an in-law.

5. To Ward Off Negativity

Basic Candle Spell and Correspondences

Day: Saturday

Hour: 1st/8th hour after sunrise; 3rd/10th hour after sunset

Planet: Saturn

Moon Phase: waning, to banish negativity

Color: black

Herbs: comfrey, slippery elm, belladonna (Saturn); basil, myrrh, rosemary (protection); paprika, thyme, garlic (wards off malevolent energy)

Oil: sandalwood

Incense: sandalwood

Stone: red jasper

Number: 8

Letters: h, q, z

Symbols: the triple ring, the pentagram

When you feel that you're being undermined by a wave of negativity, either emanating from an individual or from a set of circumstances, pull out this spell. Create your sacred space and dress a black candle, using the correspondences above. To the cauldron flame you can add a slip of paper on which you've written out the name of an individual or the surrounding circumstances that are raining on your parade and showering you with negativity.

Burn this paper and send the negative energy fleeing. No one will be harmed with this spell; energy will just be moved around – to your advantage.

Banishing Spells

I. Basic Candle Spell and Correspondences
Day: Tuesday

Hour: 1st/8th hour after sunrise; 3rd/10th hour after sunset

Planet: Mars

Moon Phase: waning/dark

Color: red, orange, black

Herbs: dragon's blood, yarrow (arrowroot), cloves, St. John's Wort

Oils/Potions/Powder: Banishing Powder, Mars Astrological Oil

Incense: patchouli

Number: 9

Letters: i, r

Symbols: Mars, an image of the person/thing you wish to banish

Whether it's an individual or a set of circumstances that you wish to banish from your life, you can use the correspondences above to dress a spell candle and craft your magic. If it's a person you wish to be rid of, use their image, signature or a name paper to burn in your spell candle. If it's a set of circumstances you wish to banish, write out on a sheet of paper exactly what it is you want gone, and burn this paper in the flame of your dressed candle.

When this spell is complete, you will want to be rid of the remnants as soon as possible, and you will want them deposited as far from you and your home as is practical. The idea is that you are sending something 'away', and so highlight this fact through the energy of your magic and the last action of this spell.

2. Ditch It Quick Spell
There's someone/something you want to be rid of – fast. You don't have time for long-drawn-out rituals; you don't have time

to wait for the moon or the energy of any particular planets. It may seem impulsive, but something tells you that it's necessary for your own safety, well-being, or sanity.

Let's do it.

Add a large spoonful of Banishing Powder to a jar of Four Thieves Vinegar. To this bottle you will also add a slip of paper with your target's name upon it, a photo, or a name paper. If it's a situation that you wish to banish, add a small slip of paper explaining what the situation is.

Shake up the bottle. Put it in a black cloth bag, and tie the bag up with a black cord, tying three knots in the cord. Hide this bag somewhere safe for three days, then remove it from its hiding place and bury it off your property.

Hexing, Cursing, Binding

1. Return to Sender
Basic Candle Spell and Correspondences

This spell is for anyone who thinks they are deliberately being targeted by someone who is sending out negative energy, intentions, harmful wishes, and such. You don't have to be 100% sure in this case that a specific person is guilty of this activity, for if they are innocent, the energy will not go to them. This spell will return the negative energy to the one who is guilty of sending it, even if you don't know who this person is.

The Correspondences

Day: Tuesday

Hour: 1st/8th hour after sunrise; 3rd/10th hour after sunset

Planet: Mars

Moon Phase: waning, to send away

Color: black

Herbs: fennel, pepper – return to sender; ginger – wards off negativity

Oil: Mars Astrological Oil

Incense: sandalwood
Stone: red jasper
Number: 9
Letters: i, r
Symbols: Runes – 'algiz', protects and shields; 'thorn',
    neutralizes foes; Odin's Cross – place this sigil with your
    name on it over the name of your enemy

Use these correspondences to create your own candle spell that is
unique to your situation, using personal effects or objects that are
related somehow to your experience. Cast a circle, call your
quarters, ground yourself, clearing your mind in order to be able
to work the magic. Focus on the energy that you are sending
away, and note that you may physically experience a weight
being lifted from your body as this negative energy races
outward.

2. A Hex

Okay, gray witches, hang onto your pointy black hats; we're
bringing out the big guns. This is the type of magic you have to
be strong enough to work so as not to be swallowed alive by its
energy. You have to be absolutely 100% sure that you want to do
this. You cannot change your mind afterwards and then go
whining to the universe because you regret what you did...it will
be too late.

Read thoroughly through these words so you fully understand the consequences and what your life will become, should
you decide to use this spell.

The Correspondences
Day: Saturday
Hour: 1st/8th hour after sunrise; 3rd/10th hour after sunset
Planet: Saturn
Color: black
Herbs: tobacco, garlic, arrowroot, morning glory vines (devil's

guts), nightshade and hemlock[5]

Oil/Potions/Powder: cemetery dirt, Goofer Dust, Banishing Powder – if this be your intention

Incense: dragon's blood

Stone: dark stones, black stones, heavy stones whose energy sinks within the earth

Number: 9

Letters: i, r

Symbols: the symbol for Saturn; an inverted pentacle; symbols relating to any of the dark gods/goddesses that you choose to work with; an inverted crucifix

Items needed:

1. A black silk bag
2. A black ribbon, approx. 12"–15" long
3. An image of your target and any personal effects from this person that you can get your hands on – the more, the better. Otherwise, you'll have to settle for a name paper.
4. Two pieces of parchment or paper with the written spell upon them – one in the witch's alphabet
5. Morning glory vines – highly recommended
6. Cobwebs
7. The carcass of a dead spider – it would be even better if you had three

The spell:
'I hex you, I hex you, I hex you,
From the bowels of the earth;
That my hex shall give birth
To a terrible curse.

'I hex you, I hex you, I hex you,

Through the dark powers that be;
That your soul shall never be free
Of this terrible curse.

I hex you, I hex you, I hex you;
So mote it be;
That you will know sadness and sorrow
And continuous misery.'

Cast your circle widdershins and call up the Watchtowers to guard your sacred space, perhaps even leaving a special token at each of the four quarters relating to that element.

Fold the spell paper written in the Witches' Alphabet three times, then tie it up with the black ribbon and spit on it. Add this to the black silk bag.

You will take the morning glory vine and bind the image of your target, all the while chanting this portion of the spell:

'I hex you, I hex you, I hex you,
From the bowels of the earth;
That my hex shall give birth
To a terrible curse.'

When you have finished binding the image, spit on it and add it to the black bag.

Add the cobwebs to the bag.

If you have one spider's carcass, add it to the black bag now while reciting the complete spell – this you can read from the other spell paper. If you have three spider's carcasses, read one verse for each carcass as you add it to the black bag. Then burn this spell paper in the flames of the black candle. Add the candle wax and ashes to the black bag after it's cooled down.

Seal this bag by tying it up with black ribbon, tying three knots in the ribbon. You will hang this token in a dark and dingy location, where it shall stay in secret, gathering dust and power and strength. It shall develop a life and intelligence of its own.

You shall never open it or set it free; for if you do, you will unleash what's in this bag on anyone within its reach.

You will spend the rest of your life making sure that this 'thing' stays safe in its secret place, that no one shall disturb it and fall prey to the powerful curse it has become.

If you are not prepared to make this kind of commitment – *do not cast this spell!*

3. A Binding

If someone is causing misery and complications in your life and you'd like nothing more than to literally hog-tie them to stop their actions, this is the spell for you. Although you can't very well physically drag them through the street by their hair and tie them to a tree, you can bind them magically with almost the same effect, and sometimes the magical binding will be an even worse punishment.

The Correspondences

Day: Saturday

Hour: 1st/8th hour after sunrise; 3rd/10th hour after sunset

Planet: Saturn

Moon Phase: waning or dark moon

Color: black

Herbs: pepper, cloves, cayenne pepper

Oil/Potions/Powder: Four Thieves Vinegar

Incense: patchouli or dragon's blood

Items needed:

1. Three ribbons each 3 feet long; two of these ribbons will be black, and the third will be a color that corresponds with your target, perhaps the color of their birth stone
2. Your black candle, dressed and ready to burn
3. Your incense

When the time is right and the magical stage has been set, seat yourself comfortably within your sacred space; ground and center.

Holding these ribbons together, as if they were a single ribbon, you are going to tie six knots – the first beginning the binding, and the last sealing it. As you tie these knots, you will recite a chant for each one, all the while retaining focus on your intentions.

The spell:

First Knot:

'I bind you now,
from feet to brow.'

Second Knot:

'I bind your mind,
that your thoughts may be frozen.'

Third Knot:

'I bind your actions,
that you may be impotent.'

Fourth Knot:

'I bind your tongue,
that you may not speak ill of anyone.'

Fifth Knot:

'I bind your power,
that you may be helpless.'

Sixth Knot:

'I bind you now,
from feet to brow.'

When the knots are tied and the spell complete, you can do one of two things with this knotted ribbon: You can burn it in the flame of the black candle and bury the remains of the spell in the earth; or you can put this knotted ribbon in a bag and keep it tucked away in a secret place.

4. Binding Negative Behavior

So you don't have a problem with an individual in general – you are just having a hard time living with a negative aspect of someone's behavior. Perhaps what they insist on doing is harmful to themselves or to people around them; either way, it has to stop.

You're going to bind this person's behavior, their actions, without actually binding the individual him/herself.

Set the magical stage with the appropriate candles, colors, herbs, stones, etc., to suit the particular situation, individual, and behavior you are addressing.

Items needed:

1. A good length of black ribbon, at least 3 feet
2. A piece of parchment or paper and a pen
3. A straight pin
4. Any item(s) you feel may carry the energy of this situation or the target – place them around the candles

Ground and center yourself in this special place, at this special time; and when you feel ready to begin, take the pen and paper and write out in your own words, to whatever extent you must, a description of the behavior that you are going to bind and the consequences that it's having on people.

With this deed done, roll the paper up in a tight scroll. Take the black ribbon, and at one end, begin the binding by wrapping the ribbon around the parchment roll – slowly, deliberately, chanting the spell as you go – until the entire ribbon is used up and the scroll is hidden beneath it.

The spell:
'I bind your behavior,
You must do as I say.
It ceases upon
This very day.'

Secure the ribbon with the straight pin.

Keep this scroll hidden in a special bag or box in a safe place. When the negative behavior has ceased, bury it in the earth.

5. Freeze Thy Enemy

When someone is being a real stinker – tearing around and disrupting people's lives, destroying reputations, creating false and misleading impressions, and otherwise making a total ass of themselves – it's time to put the brakes on. We're going to do this by literally containing the essence of this person in a sealed jar of water and freezing it solid. What better way to put a halt to someone's frenetic destructive energy!

Items needed:

1. A small glass jar with a screw-on lid
2. A photo of your target, personal effects, their signature, or a name paper
3. Sharp objects – nails, razor blades, pins and needles, shards of broken glass, etc.

(The last items listed are not absolutely required to cast this spell. They're just a little something extra to insure that the culprit feels the full brunt of their actions and the repercussions coming their way. It's the gray witch coming out in me.)

This is one of those spells I've cast in the kitchen, right at the table and near the freezer. It's a no-nonsense 'get 'er done' kind of spell that doesn't require a lot of fancy preparation or staging.

Fill the glass jar with the photo and personal effects for this hard-skulled nitwit. Add the little extra 'niceties' to it, one item at a time, possibly voicing your honest opinion of this individual and their actions as you go. Fill the jar about half full of water, maybe a little more, making sure that you've left plenty of room for expansion. Screw the lid on good and tight.

Place the jar in the freezer and slam the door shut.

The deed is done.

6. Feel My Wrath Spell

This spell is used to direct your negative energy onto an enemy. It might be compared to a physical punch in the face, and it will be felt just as keenly.

Items needed:

1. A black candle – taper or votive
2. Personal effects of the target if possible, but a photo or name paper will do
3. Dress the candle with oil and Goofer Dust

You will cast your circle widdershins for this one, and you will call the quarters to guard it. Light the elemental and altar candles so you have plenty of light, as well as an incense of your choice. You'll want to make sure that you're going to be comfortable, because you're going to be here for a while. Place a couple pillows or cushions on the floor, near the altar, if you wish.

Amidst the flickering light, protected within the circle, carve your enemy's name upon the candle. Place this candle in a cast-iron cauldron or another fireproof container, putting the image of the target or their name paper beneath it. If you have any personal effects from this individual, place them in the cauldron as well.

Ground and center. You're going to have to still your mind of outside influences and really concentrate to successfully cast this spell.

Light the black candle.

Focus on every ounce of negative feelings you have for this individual and literally gather it up and send it into the cauldron, where it in turn will be sent to the target.

If you are able to focus and direct this energy successfully, the target will feel it. Wherever this individual may be, they will become abruptly uncomfortable. They may become extremely nervous and paranoid, feeling as though they're being watched. They may tremble, shiver, or even become nauseous.

The target's discomfort will continue until the candle has burned out. However, the unnerving effects of what they have experienced will stay with them for quite some time.

The last step to this spell is extremely important:

Dispose of the remnants of this spell *off* your property. Take a little drive and find a secluded spot to dump the candle wax/ashes. Go home and smudge the room you used to cast this spell.

7. Divide and Conquer

This spell is for the witch who finds herself the victim of 'pack mentality'. She not only has to deal with a single individual who has decided to make her an enemy, but a group of people, all feeding on each other's negativity. This is the perfect spell for anyone dealing with a group of bullies.

Items needed:

1. One white candle – pillar or taper
2. Dress this candle with oil, sage, and rosemary
3. Elemental candles set at the quarters
3. A sheet of paper and a pen
4. Scissors

After the preliminaries are set – the circle cast, quarters called, candles and incense lit – sit down in the center of your circle. Take the pen and begin writing the names of the individuals in this group upon this paper. Do not write them in neat orderly rows or columns; write them helter-skelter, all over the paper, upside down and sideways.

Take the scissors and cut the names out so that each name is on an individual piece of paper. Pile these slips of paper on the altar, before the white candle, and recite this spell:

'I break you apart,
I split your heart.
Divided you shall be.
I dissolve your connections,
By the awful, awesome power
Of three times three.'

You will take the name papers and disperse them around the circle, burning one at each of the elements. If you only have two names, then by all means, burn them at opposite quarters. If you have several names, more than four, that's okay too; just keep going around the circle, burning name papers at each elemental candle you come to. The idea is that you are dispersing their energy.

Gather up the ashes from the name papers and, on a windy day, scatter these ashes to the wind.

To enhance this spell:

1. I've substituted the sage and rosemary with something a bit sharper: Banishing Powder, cayenne pepper, black pepper, or Four Thieves Vinegar.

2. If you can wait – and sometimes you can't – cast this spell on a Tuesday, using the energy of Mars; or on Saturday, using the energy of Saturn.

3. Cast this spell on a waning moon to disperse the group energy.

4. An ulterior action would be to bind them so tightly together that it has the effect of breaking them apart. This opens the door for all kinds of interesting options.

Breaking the Spell

1. Bind Me Not

If you suspect that you are the victim of a binding, don't panic. There are ways around someone else's magic – sometimes. You are going to gather the necessary ingredients, gird your loins for a seven-day ordeal, and free yourself from the ties that bind.

Items needed:

1. Command and Compel Oil
2. Seven small squares of paper and a pen
3. A white pillar candle
4. Herbs: sage, rosemary, hyssop
5. Sandalwood incense

First, you will set up an altar space that you can leave to sit for the duration of a seven-day period. You might want this in an unobtrusive part of the house, out of the way and out of sight.

The spell:

You are going to anoint the white pillar candle with the Commanding Oil, and place it in the center of your altar. This altar will be laden with dried or fresh bunches of herbs rich with cleansing energy – sage, rosemary, and hyssop. Every evening, while casting this spell, you might want to set to burn a dried pinch of these herbs in a small cauldron on a charcoal disk; and along with this, you will light sandalwood incense.

Every evening, for seven evenings, you will take a square of paper and write upon it the following words, anoint it with the Commanding Oil, and burn it in the flame of the white pillar candle. Every evening, for seven evenings, you will then gather these ashes and place them in a small bowl.

The words:
'Tit for tat,
This for that;
I undo the ties that bind.

Unwind, unwind, unwind;
Three times three,
Set me free.
Tit for tat,
This for that.'

On the seventh evening, after you have burned the last piece of paper, you will gather together all of the remnants from this spell – the ashes from the spell paper, the ashes from the herbs you've been burning, the ash from your incense, whatever's left of the pillar candle, and anything else on your altar that would be considered the remains of this spell...and you will dispose of these items as quickly as possible, as far away from your property as is reasonable.

When you return home from this venture, take a cleansing bath and sleep peacefully upon this night, in the knowledge that you are free.

2. Reverse the Curse

One of the most common and well-known ways to break your own spell is to re-gather all the ingredients that you used when you first cast it – *and do the entire thing in reverse.*

For some spells, this may work; and for other spells, it will not.

Did you do something that you regret, perhaps perform a spell of black magic in a fit of anger? Although there is no guarantee of reversing your spell, if you feel bad or desperate enough – give it a shot. Then hold your breath with the universe and see what happens.

This is a reminder: think twice before casting negative magic, or any magic at all; don't act rashly in anger – this never works, even on a mundane level; consider the consequences and realize that once the energy has been turned loose, the deed is done.

To anyone who needs this spell, I wish you success in your endeavor.

3. Breaking Another Witch's Spell

This spell is going to incorporate the use of knot magic. After preparing the ribbon for this spell and tying the necessary knots, you're going to 'cut to the heart of the matter'.

Items needed:

1. A black ribbon, approximately 2 feet long
2. A pair of scissors – your bolline knife would be better

Cast your circle widdershins for this spell. We're going to be working magic in reverse, and we're going to be tampering with another witch's magic – she may or may not feel this interference with her energy.

Bolster the perimeter of your sacred space with white candles and a protective incense: patchouli, or something else that's 'earthy'. Call the quarters to stand guard, to protect you from any backlash of incoming negative energy. I would heap the altar with black candles and a plethora of protective herbs – either large dried or fresh bunches, or small bowls of ground herbs or their seeds – herbs such as anise, bay, bloodroot, fennel, garlic, mugwort, or hyssop. Put a small bunch of these herbs in a cauldron to burn.

When all is ready, seat yourself in the center of this circle, amidst the flickering candle flames and smoldering incense. Take up the black ribbon. Hold it in the smoke of the herbs, slowly, languidly, allowing your mind to wrap itself around the spell that you are going to break and the witch who cast it.

At one end of this ribbon, tie the first knot to represent the spell and the witch who cast it, saying:

'I tie to this, thy ribbon of magic, a knot of one;

That ye may know what I have done.'

At the other end of this black ribbon, tie a knot to represent yourself, saying:

'I tie to this, thy ribbon of magic, a knot of two;

That all you've done will come back on you.'

Take your time – hold the ribbon, chant, sway, float, dance, caress the ribbon, close your eyes, lose yourself...and feel the energy rise. When it is at fever pitch, take up the scissors or knife and cut the ribbon in the center, severing the pathway of energy between yourself, the other witch, and the spell she cast.

Bury this ribbon in the earth, in some godforsaken place, burying the energy and power of this witch right along with the ribbon.

Notes

1 http://www.youtube.com/results?search_query=african+witch+hunts&aq=f
2 Quote from Benjamin Cardoza
http://en.wikiquote.org/wiki/Benjamin_N._Cardozo
3 Both hellebore and tansy are poisonous.
4 Nightshade is poisonous and can be absorbed through the skin. Handle it with gloved hands only – if you handle it at all! If you burn it, which I wouldn't advise, don't inhale the fumes.
5 Since nightshade and hemlock are both poisonous, I suggest you look upon their inclusion in this list as an interesting historical footnote – and then work with the nonpoisonous herbs listed.

Moon Books invites you to begin or deepen your encounter with Paganism, in all its rich, creative, flourishing forms.